Warming the Climate for Women in Academic Science

Warming the Climate for Women in Academic Science

Angela B. Ginorio

AAC&U

Association of American Colleges and Universities
Program on the Status and Education of Women
Washington, D.C.

Published by the Association of American Colleges and Universities,
1818 R Street, NW, Washington, DC 20009

ISBN 0-911696-63-6

Cover illustrations:

Maria Sibylla Merian (German, 1647–1717). *Dissertation in Insect Generations and Metamorphosis in Surinam*, 1719. Plates 1, 31, and 37. Bound volume of seventy-two hand-colored engravings, 2nd edition. The National Museum of Women in the Arts. Gift of Wallace and Wilhelmina Holladay.

During the early period of her life Maria Sibylla Merian conducted scientific research on the life cycles of insects and also produced flower paintings and drawings for private patrons. She collected insect eggs, caterpillars, cocoons, chrysalises, and adults of each species and studied their eating habits and evolution. Her discoveries confounded the popular belief of her day that most insects emerged spontaneously from dirt and mud. She published her research in 1679 and 1683 as *The Wonderful Transformation of Caterpillars and [Their] Singular Plant Nourishment.* A third volume was published post-humously in 1717. The book catalogues 186 European moths, butterflies, and other insects. The format was revolutionary, showing on a single page each insect in all stages of metamorphosis, on or near a plant she had learned was its favorite. Her design became a model for zoological and botanical illustrations.

In 1699 Merian traveled to Surinam, where for two years she collected and raised insects, made extensive notes and drawings, and interviewed the native population concerning local customs, especially regarding the uses of plants. Her research from this trip was published as *Insects of Surinam* (1705) and in a second edition as *Dissertations in Insect Generation and Metamorphosis in Surinam* (1719).

TABLE OF CONTENTS AND ILLUSTRATIONS

Illustrations

The first version of this paper was presented as a lecture in the University of Washington's School of Oceanography. I would like to thank C. J. Beagle, Devamonie Naidoo, and the other graduate students who started this conversation at our campus. The title for this paper flows from that talk and from the joint concerns of those graduate students: the "chilly climate" they were feeling in their school and the "global warming" that is such a central topic for oceanographers. The "Warming the Climate for Women in Science" lecture was part of a series initiated by the dean to bring the concerns of the students to the attention of the whole school. While any deliberate attempt to warm the climate would be considered potentially dangerous to the survival of those species that had been nurtured by the current global climate, introducing changes to the cultural climate is what human history has been all about.

The staff of the Northwest Center for Research on Women has supported this work. In particular I would like to thank my research assistant Michelle Elekonich for help with the literature search and the drafting of the final version of this manuscript and Re-Cheng Tsang and Terry Marshall for general assistance. Many thanks to all the people who read this manuscript at various stages and offered helpful suggestions: Elaine Seymour from the Bureau of Sociological Research at the University of Colorado; Suzanne Brainard and Kate Noble from the University of Washington; and Caryn McTighe Musil, director of the Association of American Colleges and Universities' Program on the Status and Education of Women—many thanks not only for a very keen editorial pen but also for her enthusiasm for this project. At AAC&U I would also like to thank other staff who worked with grace under pressure to prepare this monograph: Debra Humphreys, editor of *On Campus with Women;* Cindy Olson, production editor; and Amy Wajda, assistant desktop editor, for designing and producing *Warming the Climate* and for locating the elegant Maria Sibylla Merian illustrations that appear on the cover.

I would also like to thank all of the people who responded to the various requests for information: Helen Remick of the University of Washington; Louise Fitzgerald of the University of Illinois; Mary Frank Fox of the Georgia Institute of Technology; David Targan of Brown University; Karen Arnold of Boston University; Bonnie Spanier of the State University of New York–Albany; the members of the Feminists in Science and Technology (FIST) e-mail list, Jen Cohen in particular; and my colleagues in the Cross-University Research in Engineering and Science (CURIES) group: Cinda-Sue Davis and Carol Hollenshead from the University of Michigan, Barbara Lazarus from Carnegie-Mellon University, and Paula Rayman, formerly of the Pathways Project at the Center for Research on Women at Wellesley College.

Finally, I would like to dedicate this to the memory of Betty Vetter, founder of the Commission on Professionals in Science and Technology. Her tireless efforts provided us with the invaluable data that over the years allowed us to track women's status in science and engineering. She died while the final draft of this manuscript was being prepared. Without all of them, my daughter Emilia Beatriz—who at age six thinks that "math is fun" and "science is cool"— would not stand much of a chance of continuing to enjoy math and science into adulthood.

—*Angela B. Ginorio*
Northwest Center for Research on Women

A reasonable objective for the education of women and minority students is that they have a *fair chance to succeed* in graduate school; that the *feedback loop of lowered expectations* based on sex or race, leading to lowered *self-image* and finally to lower *performance*, be broken by *conscious action* by faculty and students. (Emphasis added.)

—*Sheila E. Widnall, in "AAAS Presidential Lecture: Voices from the Pipeline,"* Science 241 (1988): 1740–43. *At the time, Widnall was Abby Rockefeller Mauze Professor of Aeronautics and Astronautics at the Massachusetts Institute of Technology. Currently she is Secretary of the Air Force.*

When Sheila E. Widnall gave her presidential lecture, "Voices from the Pipeline," to the American Association for the Advancement of Science (AAAS) in 1988, she insisted on the centrality of an issue that the scientific community as a whole saw as peripheral. The climate created in science, mathematics, and engineering (SME), Widnall argued, was fundamental to the vitality and intellectual robustness of the field. Evidence had been mounting that the climate in science itself was affecting who was attracted to science, who stayed, and who ultimately chose it as a profession. Since Widnall's speech, it has become harder to deny that the climate—or culture—of science has been chilly to women, ethnic minorities, and people with disabilities.

This paper continues and updates the discussion Widnall started by reviewing research findings in three areas:

♦ numbers of women participating in science education and careers;

♦ evidence of pre-college patterns for girls and women in science and math; and

♦ studies on how women are faring in college as undergraduate and graduate students and as faculty members.

In addition, the paper:

♦ briefly reviews some of the major institutional responses to these concerns;

♦ provides recommendations for action that can be taken by undergraduate and graduate students, faculty members, administrators, and professional organizations; and

♦ includes a resource section of bibliographies, organizations, and special contacts for more information.

AN ALLEGORY

Imagine that academia is like a plant collector intent on cultivating plants from diverse kinds of climates in an excellent conservatory.

Facilities are built, employees are hired, and field collectors are contacted to obtain the best and most diverse specimens. The field collectors go out to their respective locales and secure the very best specimens they can find, then prepare them carefully for the long trip back to the conservatory.

When they arrive, some of the plants look weakened by the transport—but most look healthy. The plants are quickly placed in sites that were prepared for them. But soon after, mysteriously, many of the plants begin to wilt. After a while some look as if they won't survive. Concerned, the collector wonders, "What's wrong with the plants?" The field collectors answer the query, "The plants were carefully selected as the best specimens in each of the sites." Still puzzled, yet determined to find out what is wrong with the plants, the conservatory staff calls the transportation company: "Did something happen on the way?" They learn that, indeed, for a few of the shipments the conditions were colder than ideal, and that one shipment was not watered consistently.

While the staff is processing this information, some plants start to die. Pressed by the urgency of the situation, the chief collector calls a meeting and for the first time asks, "Is it something we're doing?" The collector then asks each of the gardeners, "How do you care for the plants you are responsible for?" The collector receives three kinds of answers: "I treat them all the same," says the first group, which represents the majority of caretakers. "I only feed and water the ones that are thriving. Why waste resources?" responds a second group of caretakers. The third and smallest group replies, "I try to provide what each plant needs."

When the collector examines plants under the care of each group of employees, only the plants given the third style of care, the responsive style, are flourishing. Not one had died. While few plants died among those cared for by the first group (using the sameness style), many plants were not thriving. About one-half of the plants in the middle group ("only the thriving ones" style) had died.[1]

INTRODUCTION

This allegory can be applied to many aspects of university-level science, mathematics, and engineering education. First, the story can be read with an emphasis on the outcome of the interaction between caretakers and plants. Read that way, the focus is on individual institutions, where in the not-so-distant past most employees, faculty members, teaching assistants, and advisors would have focused on students who were thriving. This style of caretaking was typically applied to a student body without much diversity—mostly male, mostly White, mostly middle-class. By contrast, today's students are far more diverse in terms of race, ethnicity, gender, age, sexual orientation, class, and disabilities. A style of teaching that still does not work for more homogeneous groups of students—as indicated by high dropout rates—will not succeed in retaining the more diverse population of today.[2]

> **Not so long ago, the presence of anyone but White men in an SME classroom was seen as "the problem."**

One can also read the story with a focus on the definition of "the problem." Read that way, we can see how much the institutional climate of science has changed. Not so long ago, the presence of anyone but White men in an SME classroom was seen as "the problem." Under those conditions, the caretakers would not have asked, "What is wrong with the plants?" but, "What is wrong?" The answer would have been, "Certain plants do not belong here." Today, many scientists, engineers, and mathematicians are asking, "Is the problem something we are doing?" Because they begin with that question, they offer solutions that focus on what individuals and institutions can do to make a difference.

For some time, information about White women, women and men of color, and women and men with disabilities[3] has prompted the institution-centered query. Some of this information comes from data collected on numbers of participants in science education and careers. Data on numbers of participants clearly show differential participation by women and men in various fields of science and across the professional lifetime. Some data come also from surveys and other studies of samples of science students and scientists. The surveys and qualitative studies explore factors that may account for this differential participation.

Much of what institutions can do to provide solutions can be included under the rubric of climate. Climate has been defined as the prevailing condition affecting life and activity. In an academic setting the climate is set by the expectations and past experiences of students, faculty members, and staff; by the history of the institution; and by the behaviors and goals that are expected and rewarded.

University of Colorado–Boulder

The climate of science at the under-graduate level is characterized by a selection process that relies heavily on quantitative measures at entry into college and on introductory courses meant to weed out students from science once in college; by a training process that is impersonal and often competitive; and by a life-style that puts a premium on long hours of work.[1] At the graduate level another issue is added, especially for those women in physics and engi-neering: the isolation that comes from being one of a few in a given department at any time, and having very few—if any—women on the faculty who could serve as role mod-els.[2] That isolation is compounded by the difficulty of finding supportive mentors.[3] Some women graduate stu-dents and many women faculty members also face concerns over the integration of family and academic work.[4] These aspects of the climate of science are often cited as explana-tions for women's disproportionately low representation in some fields of science.

Interestingly, these aspects of sci-ence are becoming troublesome for men, too, as evidenced by the 1992 conference, "Changing the Culture of Science," sponsored by the National Science Foundation and eight Univer-sity of California research centers in physics and computer science. This conference focused on issues of eth-nicity as well as gender. During one address, Walter Massey, at the time the director of the National Science Foundation, commented that the increasing numbers of male scientists with working spouses and young

children, as well as changing mores about the father's role in childrearing, had made issues of childcare, flexible time, and parental leave a concern for men. Similar discussions occurred during the past year in scientific elec-tronic networks such as the Young Scientists Network.

Scientists and individuals inter-ested in the health of science and in science and engineering education are coming to recognize what many

women in science and scholars inter-ested in how women experience sci-ence education and careers have been saying for the past decade: changing the chilly climate that has kept women away from scientific fields is a necessity. This necessity grows not only from issues of equity for under-represented groups, but also from the awareness that science must change if it is to adapt to the needs of society today and in the next century.

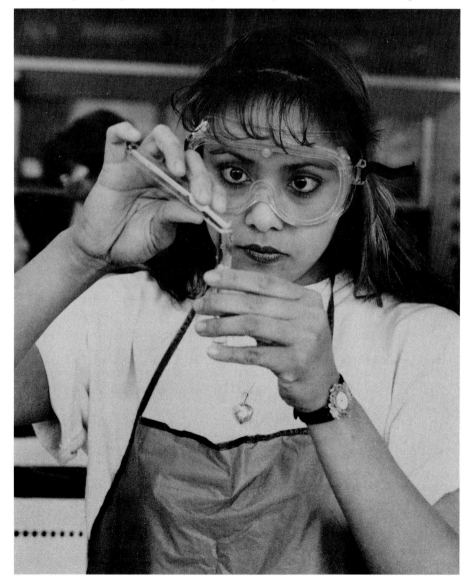

California State University–Long Beach

3

Except in the biosciences, women have not achieved parity even at the bachelor's level in any of the natural science fields, although they earned a majority of all bachelor's degrees by 1983.

—Betty M. Vetter, "Women in Science, Mathematics and Engineering: Myth and Realities" (paper for the CURIES Conference on Women in Science, Mathematics and Engineering, Wellesley, Mass., May 1994), 8.

A historical review of the numbers of women students in science, mathematics, and engineering indicates that the dramatic gains in women's enrollment and graduation in most SME fields started in the late 1960s. But it was not until the mid-1970s that the percentage of Ph.D. degrees awarded to women in science matched the percentage granted in the 1920s.[1] While there is no doubt that women have continued to increase their numbers in all the natural science fields, over the past ten years the increase in bachelor's degrees awarded to women occurred gradually and has reached a plateau or even decreased slightly in fields such as the computer sciences, natural sciences, and engineering.[2] Some of the increases in women's participation have been magnified by the concurrent decrease in numbers of men seeking degrees in these areas. For example, from 1986 to 1991 a 25 percent drop occurred in the total number of bachelor's degrees awarded in the natural sciences and engineering.

The percentage of master's degrees earned by women in most science fields is similar to the percentage of bachelor's degrees (27 percent versus 22 percent); the big drop occurs at the doctoral level. In 1992, 2,483 women received Ph.D.'s in natural

science and engineering fields for a total of 26.3 percent of all doctoral degrees awarded to American citi-

Only seven universities in the United States in the past ten years awarded more than 100 Ph.D.'s to students of color in mathematics, engineering, and the natural sciences combined.

zens. But considering that almost 8,000 Ph.D. degrees were awarded to foreign nationals that same year, and

that the vast majority of those were men, women's representation shrinks to 14.4 percent of the total number of Ph.D.'s granted that year in science and engineering fields. There are also major differences by field in the numbers of women receiving Ph.D.'s, ranging from 13.7 percent in engineering to 44.7 percent in biology.

When the numbers of SME degrees awarded to ethnic minority American women in 1992 are broken down by groups, we find that the actual numbers are miniscule for all groups except Asian Americans: 11 Ph.D.'s granted in science, mathematics, and engineering to American Indian women, 34 to African American women, 71 to Latinas, and 143 to Asian American women.[3] Such numbers only hint at the relative isolation of each of these individuals as they went through their training in departments with small numbers of women and even smaller numbers of women of color. Only seven universities in the United States in the past ten years awarded more than 100 Ph.D.'s to students of color in mathematics, engineering, and the natural sciences combined. In contrast, more than 30,000 degrees have been awarded to White students in mathematics, engineering, and the natural sciences in the past ten years, with 146 universities awarding more than 100 Ph.D.'s in these fields and 18 of those universities awarding over 1,000 Ph.D.'s.[4]

Among women in faculty positions, the picture is much the same everywhere we look: the higher the rank, the lower the proportion of women, and the higher the status of the coeducational institution, the lower the proportion of women. The number of women varies by fields, from 40 percent in medical sciences to 4 percent in engineering and 3 percent in physics.[5] The lack of a qualified pool has been cited as a reason for women's absence in the tenure ranks. But numbers are not the only reason for their absence, as the following examples illustrate:

◆ A higher proportion of women than men are in non-tenure track academic positions.[6]

◆ Between 1985 and 1990 the number of female full professors in chemistry increased from 3 percent to 4 percent.[7]

◆ There are only four tenured women in mathematics in the top ten departments in the United States.[8]

◆ One-half of the doctoral programs in physics in the United States have no women faculty members.[9]

◆ In a survey of representation of women physicists in university science faculties in twenty countries, the United States tied for last place with Korea.[10]

◆ Between 1949 and 1987 only thirty-four African American women had earned Ph.D. degrees in mathematics.[11]

Department	Total	Percent Women		
		Assistant Professor	Associate Professor	Full Professor
Biological Sciences	18.5	25.1	21.2	10.4
Engineering	4.0	9.9	2.4	0.3
Math/Statistics	23.0	26.8	15.4	9.9
Physical Sciences	8.8	18.2	6.4	4.4
All Fields	28.6	37.7	25.7	13.7

Source: Astin and Sax, Table 3.

Weighted N for all women = 101,620 (original N = 9,933)
Weighted N for total sample = 355,715 (original N = 31, 576)

Figure 1. *Women Faculty in the Sciences: Department of Current Faculty Appointment by Academic Rank (weighted data).*

The women who choose science, engineering, or mathematics as a major in college have already been deeply influenced by their K–12 educational experiences. In both single-sex and coeducational classrooms, the expectations of teachers and parents have a strong effect on the education of girls.[1] There is some evidence that teachers' beliefs regarding the appropriateness of science and math for boys and girls are more influenced by sex-role stereotypes than are students' own perceptions.[2] Thus, instead of liberating young girls from narrow expectations, the educational setting often reinforces stereotypes about gender-appropriate behavior, interests, and occupations. In coeducational settings, sexism most often takes the form of differential treatment, while in single-sex settings, sexism most often appears as undemanding instruction that fosters girls' academic dependence.[3]

The outcomes of this system are many. For instance, while both boys and girls in seventh grade have positive perceptions of science and the same level of interest in careers in science, by eleventh grade girls have dropped significantly below boys on both measures. Moreover, this drop in self-perception of science ability and interest in science is greatest for White girls.[4] The little data that exists on American Indian students suggests gender socialization has a great effect on those for these girls as well.[5] In all cases parents' attitude and support can make a great difference in the outcome.

In mathematics there is no difference in the achievement scores of boys and girls at age nine.[6] While Whites score higher than either African American or Latina and

Latino students, the gap widens as students move through the educational system. It must be noted that this is not a universal outcome. Non-White girls in Hawaii, for example, outperform boys in math, and

> While both boys and girls in seventh grade have positive perceptions of science and the same level of interest in careers in science, by eleventh grade girls have dropped significantly below boys on both measures.

American students' scores are very low relative to the scores of students in other countries.[7] A meta-analysis conducted on performance in mathematics indicates that differences in problem solving favoring boys emerge in high school and are greater with samples of above-average students, although the magnitude of the

differences has diminished over the years.[8] A parallel meta-analysis of seventy studies of gender differences in attitudes and affect found that although the differences are small, they are larger in high school than in primary school, and that girls hold more negative attitudes toward mathematics than boys.[9]

Academically, girls take more life science courses and boys more physical science courses, and the gender differences observed in enrollment in mathematics courses occur for precalculus and calculus in high school.[10] The other differences between women and men who enter science and engineering fields are higher grade point averages (GPAs) and lower Scholastic Aptitude Test (SAT) scores attained by young women.[11] These relatively small differences in cognitive skills cannot account for the large differences that are perceived or for outcomes either in high school or college.[12] There are some studies, however, which indicate that pre-college preparation has positive effects, not in the choice of SME major but in the persistence within these fields. Strenta and his colleagues found pre-college preparation was an important factor in predicting persistence in science among students in Ivy League schools.[13]

In a longitudinal study of students, Ware, Steckler, and Lesserman report that men of differing abilities in mathematics choose science majors while the women who do so have a very high aptitude for math. Ethington, in a retrospective study of women, finds that math/science self-rating of ability is the highest predictor of choosing a science major.[14] In another retrospective look at students' motivations for choosing science as a college major, a striking gender difference is observed in the sample of college students interviewed by Seymour and Hewitt: women choose SME majors because of personal influences (family, high school teachers, and other significant adults), while men choose majors for perceived (not always accurate) competence in mathematics or science, anticipated financial outcomes, or because male family members are scientists or engineers.[15]

Thus, the small but consistent gaps in various areas of high school proficiency in math and science between women and men may ultimately have effects not only on colleges' admissions decisions but on students' choice of, and persistence in, SME majors. In the social environment there are also small but consistent pushes and pulls that account for the lesser likelihood of women choosing science: stereotypical expectations of parents and teachers, lower self-confidence in math and science ability, and women's greater reliance on others for motivation and encouragement. In their transit from home to college, some young women, like the plants in the allegory, are improperly nurtured. But if they make it as far as college with skills and interest in SME, their survival skills are better than average—under normal circumstances they should thrive.[16]

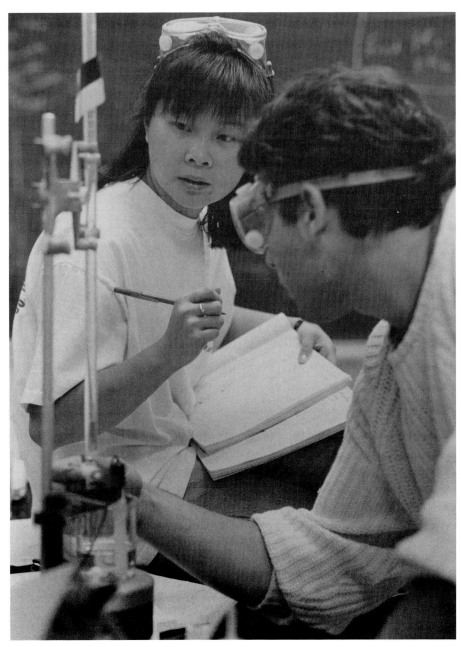

Skidmore College

Sometimes, I really doubted myself in classes....At first, I thought there were a lot of women in class; after a while, I looked around and there were only three or four. And I started wondering, "Do I really belong here?"

—*woman engineering non-switcher in Seymour and Hewitt, 409*

At this point the career comes first. Last spring I did a lot of things with graduate students....Now I see that there is potential and I think it's silly to waste it, so I want to be good at what I'm doing.

—*Sherri, bioengineering major, in Arnold*

A retrospective longitudinal study at a large public research university finds that men are more likely than women to persist in their original science or engineering major, but that they are also more likely to leave the university altogether. Women, on the other hand, are more likely to persist at the university but also to switch out of science. When grades are controlled for, women are no more likely than men to leave the university or switch out of science. However, a difference between women and men remains even after controlling for grades: women are more likely than

men to switch from their original science major to a different science major.[1] Thus, while women persist as much as men in science when GPA is controlled for, they still tend to switch from one science major to another more frequently than do their male counterparts. And while the proportion of persisters may be the same, the ratio of women to men in some fields, such as engineering, is still very low. At the University of Washington, for example, there has been only one woman for every five men among all undergraduates in engineering over the past five years.[2]

Two additional longitudinal studies examine female persistence. In a study of engineering students at the University of California–Berkeley, Humphreys and Freeland find that women leave engineering at higher rates than men, with the highest persistence shown by Chinese and Chinese American students, followed by other Asians and Asian Americans, Whites, and lastly, Latinas and Latinos.[3] In a study of four Ivy League schools (Brown University, Cornell University, Dartmouth College, and Yale University), researchers find a large persistence effect due to pre-college preparation, with more women lacking adequate preparation. When these factors are controlled for, no differences are observed between men's and women's persistence in engineering and biology, but there are differences in physical sciences and mathematics.[4] These longitudinal studies controlling for factors that can account for differential persistence are an improvement over previous studies that, using pseudo-cohorts for their samples, invariably find a lower persistence of women in engineering and science.[5]

Nonetheless, even with the additional controls, differential persistence has been found in at least one area in each of the studies. These areas tend to be the physical sciences and

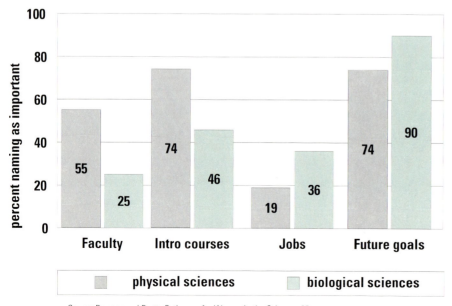

Source: Rayman and Brett, *Pathways for Women in the Sciences*, 69.

Figure 2. *Types of Science By Sources of Influence on Major among Women at Wellesley College.*

mathematics, fields where women have traditionally been underrepresented. As a result, explanations based on the culture or subject matter of some disciplines have been offered to explain women's underrepresentation. But the finding is not consistent across all settings, pointing to the culture of the department rather than, or in addition to, the field as a potential mediator in women's persistence. At Wellesley College, for example, women in the physical sciences (astronomy, chemistry, geology and physics) were more likely than students in the life sciences to have faculty contact, see college teachers as a source of support and encouragement, and report that their teachers had an influence on their career choice.[6]

While grades or pre-college preparation may be significant predictors of persistence in studies using quantitative measures, when asked directly, female students list other factors as more important in their decisions. Seymour and Hewitt's qualitative study of undergraduate students on seven campuses provides interesting data on students' motivation to stay or leave SME fields in college. An extensive listing of the reasons for leaving science includes, in descending order of importance (with percentage of women citing the reason in parentheses after):

1. other major offers better education or more interest (46 percent);
2. lack or loss of interest in SME (43 percent); and
3. rejection of SME careers and associated lifestyles (38 percent).[7]

In an ongoing longitudinal study, Brainard finds that students in engineering give reasons that strongly confirm the first two reasons given by

students in Seymour and Hewitt's study.[8] Ranked sixth out of twenty-one reasons given by men and ninth by women, discouragement or loss of confidence due to low grades is a more important reason for men (27 percent) than for women (19 percent). Inadequate high school preparation is mentioned by 15 percent of both women and men (ranking eleventh and thirteenth, respectively). Seymour and Hewitt point out that while many women choose

> **"[Y]oung women show a greater concern to make their education, their career goals, and their personal priorities fit coherently together."**
>
> *—Seymour and Hewitt*

majors influenced by the desires of significant people in their lives such as parents and teachers, they leave or stay in SME majors for their own reasons—this choice is their own.[9] Interestingly, in Brainard's study, a belief that relatives did not influence their decision was a predictor of women's level of confidence to the end of their first year.[10] A similar finding is

reported by Wiegand, Ginorio, and Brown with regard to career choices. Women involved in a single-sex science enrichment program are the least likely to report parental influences in their choice of science as a major—compared with women involved in a coeducational science enrichment program and a control group. While across all groups Asian American women were significantly more likely to mention their mother as an influence in their choice of science as a major, the Asian American women in the single-sex group were significantly less likely to identify their mothers as influencing their choice of major.[11] It would seem that first-year undergraduate women students who choose an SME major as a result of their own choice, or who are perhaps informed by non-familial influences, are more likely to persist, have confidence in their ability in SME, or select an SME career.

In judging the desirability of a major and potential career, students include considerations about how the major or career would allow for the inclusion of other significant aspects of their lives. Many women include raising children as part of their life goals; students of color also include involvement with their communities.[12] To the degree that for some students these are current responsibilities rather than potential future ones, their career choices may be further constrained. Many White women and many students of color of both sexes are less single-minded about pursuing careers than most White men.

Interestingly, Seymour and Hewitt find that male students also consider their anticipated family responsibilities in their choice of career and may persist in a major that does not have as much intrinsic interest to them but promises greater economic reward. African American women are also more likely to mention economic considerations in their reasons for persistence than are White women. While many women anticipate shouldering most childcare and child support responsibilities, this anticipation does not bind them as closely to majors of no intrinsic interest for them. These qualitative results mirror the quantitative results generated by Astin and Sax in their studies with the Cooperative Institutional Research Program.[13] Seymour and Hewitt conclude that "young women show a greater concern to make their education, their career goals, and their personal priorities fit coherently together."[14]

While Seymour and Hewitt aim for representativeness in the seven campuses in their study, Arnold has been following a group of eighty 1981 high school graduates (forty-six women, thirty-four men) who were that year's valedictorians in Illinois, of whom 19 percent were science majors and 19 percent were engineering majors in college.[15] Two of Arnold's findings are of interest to this discussion: one confirms Seymour and Hewitt's finding about the importance of family concerns for women students, and the other vividly illustrates the diminished sense of competence experienced by many women in college. Arnold reports that the women in her sample factor concerns about future family responsibilities and children into their decisions about majors and about how far to pursue their education.[16] Arnold's study also finds that the women with college GPAs similar to those of men (women's GPAs were at

| | | 1985 | | 1989 | | Percent Change | |
Self-Rating	Men	Women	Men	Women	Men	Women
Highest 10 Percent	24.4	10.8	20.9	8.7	-3.5	-2.1
Above Average	37.5	35.3	37.6	32.5	+0.1	-2.8
Average	26.9	36.1	28.4	38.3	+1.5	+2.2
Below Average	9.6	14.4	11.5	17.6	+1.9	+3.2
Lowest 10 Percent	1.6	3.4	1.6	2.9	0.0	-0.5
Mean	3.74	3.36	3.65	3.26	-0.09	-0.1
(S.D.)	(.98)	(.97)	(.98)	(.95)		

Source: Astin and Sax, Table 6.

Note: Chi-square tests indicate statistically significant gender differences ($p<.0001$) in both 1985 and 1989.
Male n=6,053
Female n=8,997

Figure 3. *Changes in Mathematical Self-Rating for Men and Women During College.*

3.7; men's, 3.6), negatively evaluate their intelligence after four years in college. None of the women, compared to 25 percent of the men, judge themselves to be "far above average" in intelligence. In contrast, similar proportions of men and women (23 percent of men and 21 percent of women) give themselves ratings of "far above average" in intelligence at the end of high school.[17] In two current samples, Brainard's longitudinal and quantitative study of engineering students, and Seymour and Hewitt's retrospective and quantitative study, the same effect is reported, with self-confidence declining significantly during the first year and not going back to entry-level values over the undergraduate college years regardless of grades.[18] For these outstanding women, college is an experience that leads to a diminished sense of competence—even in the face of their continued academic success.

A diminishing of self-confidence in math ability is also reported for a sample of almost nine thousand students by Astin and Sax, with women's confidence decreasing more than men's over four years of college.[19] But when analyzed separately for math and science majors versus other students, the data reveals that women who persist in math or science increase their self-confidence in their math ability. On the other hand, a study at the University of Michigan with undergraduate women enrolled in honors sections in math found that, in spite of high grades, women would major in math at a lower rate than men.[20] The picture that emerges from these studies suggests that small but consistent messages and behaviors reinforce sexist expectations and decrease women's overall sense of self-competence—although not their academic performance. In the absence of overt discrimination these micro-inequities help explain the differential persistence of women.[21] While hard to detect in a cross-sectional study, the disadvantage created by the accumulation of such inequities becomes evident when longitudinal or qualitative studies are pursued.

Students' experiences with sexual harassment provide a good example of how important it is to use different methods to study a phenomena. The sexual harassment that students describe in Seymour and Hewitt's report is of the pervasive, hostile-environment variety. Most harassment is carried out by peers in the classroom with the teacher's silent consent. Only 6 of 173 female students report that their teachers actively engaged in gender harassment (including demeaning comments, offensive jokes, and crude sexual remarks), and only 2 students report overt sexual harassment by teachers.[22] These results, the only specific to science education, are in agreement with other studies of undergraduates in finding gender harassment to be the most typical form of sexual harassment in the classroom. However, through the use of surveys rather than interviews, a higher number of professors or instructors are identified as engaging in these behaviors.[23] Seymour and Hewitt's observations of focus group discussions provide a possible explanation. Students speak of gender harassment incidents in ways that normalize the offensive behavior and expressed fear that complaints from women will be seen as indicating a weakness of character or of academic competence. Thus, different methodologies provide different perspectives on the same issues.

> **Small but consistent messages and behaviors reinforce sexist expectations and decrease women's overall sense of self-competence—although not their academic performance.**

and career goals, customary ways of learning, and of responding to problems, which has been built up along gender lines throughout childhood and adolescence, is suddenly brought into focus, and into practical significance. This occurs because both gender groups are entering an educational system which has evolved to support the ongoing socialization process of only one of them—White men.[24]

It appears that the daily grind of small jokes and demeaning comments as well as aloofness on the part of teachers is discouraging to the majority of women—those who stayed as well as those who switched. Seymour and Hewitt explain the process that undergraduate women experience when they enter SME fields thus:

> We posit that entry to freshman science, mathematics or engineering suddenly makes explicit, and then heightens, what is actually a long-standing divergence in the socialization experiences of young men and women. The divergence in self-perceptions, attitudes, life

THE GRADUATE EXPERIENCE

Part of the game of getting through graduate school is perceiving what the game rules are. One is not presented a list of the rules, it's up to one to divine the rules.

—*Etzkowitz et al., "Athena Unbound," 165*

I worked on five research projects as an undergraduate and graduate student and the recognition of my contributions was zero.

—*White woman research associate, M.Sc. and J.D.[1]*

In 1983, in a benchmark publication about the climate at their institution, the women graduate students and research staff at the Laboratory for Computer Science and the Artificial Intelligence Laboratory at the Massachusetts Institute of Technology felt compelled to start the concluding section of their report women in computer science at MIT with the following statement:

> Although not a generally accepted fact, the women here are as qualified as the men. In order to realize their potential, women must be given the same opportunities as men to participate in and benefit from all aspects of the professional community.[2]

Eleven years later, in their review of the literature on graduate education, Hollenshead, Wenzel, Lazarus, and Nair report that the few studies focusing on women in science and engineering at the graduate level show that women in science and engineering are still far from having the same experiences as men in graduate school.[3] They report that women take longer to achieve candidacy and degree. The data they present on completion rates for graduate students in science and engineering doctoral programs for a number of institutions show that the completion rate for women ranges from only

about 43 percent to 59 percent, compared to 52 percent and 65 percent for men in the respective institutions.[4] Some of these students may go on to other institutions to finish their degrees. But in a longitudinal study following natural sciences and engi-

> ### The thing that seems to discourage women most at the graduate level is the sense of isolation within their departments.

neering alumni (State University of New York–Stony Brook), Preston reports that women were less likely to have completed the Ph.D.—26 percent of women versus 13 percent of men.[5]

Not surprisingly, there are differences among institutions and, interestingly, women (and men) in the natural sciences are more likely to

attain the Ph.D. than are women (and men) in the social sciences or humanities.[6] While the amount of financial support in these fields may help to explain these differences, within the natural sciences women who received prestigious fellowships were not more likely to graduate than women who did not receive such funding.[7]

A study conducted at Princeton University by David Redman reports on completion rates for men and women in eleven Ph.D.-granting departments. Redman finds that women's rates of completion are equal to or better than men's in those departments in which women graduate students constituted at least 20 percent of the student body. By contrast, in departments where women graduate students constituted 15 percent or fewer, their graduation rates lagged behind those of men by 6 percent to 15 percent. With one exception, departments that had low graduation rates also had few or no women faculty members. The Princeton University study seems to suggest that a critical number of women is needed in order to ensure that women's graduation rates are at least equal to men's.[8] But as Etzkowitz, Kemelgor, Neuschatz, Uzzi, and Alonzo have argued, "attainment of a critical mass only partly resolved the dilemma of women in academic departments" (52).

Differences are found between women's and men's graduate student experiences in a number of areas. In a survey of all graduate students in science and medicine conducted by Zappert and Stansbury at Stanford University in 1987, 35 percent of the men and 24 percent of the women foresaw no difficulties in their future careers. Two-thirds of the women and one-third of the men anticipated some degree of difficulty in attempting to balance both career and family. Similarly, two-thirds of the women and a one-quarter of the men anticipated problems with the timing of children in the context of the development of their career (Figure 4). These anticipated conflicts are realistic given that more women than men reported doing housework while still in graduate school, and 50 percent of

women but only 1 percent of men stayed home with a sick child. More women than men also find it stressful to juggle multiple roles (50 percent of women and 23 percent of men).[9]

More Stanford graduate women than men reported negative experiences with their advisor (40 percent of women versus 30 percent of men), and 13 percent of women feel that the sex of their advisor had a negative impact on them compared with only 1 percent of the men. Berg and Ferber report that fewer women than men knew one or more male faculty members well (54 percent versus 78 percent), and fewer report being treated as a junior colleague by faculty members (49 percent of women versus 61 percent of men).[10] Similar results have been reported not only for women but also for international students in entomology by Pearson.[11]

Mentors can be invaluable in learning "the rules of the game." A male mentor can be supportive in many aspects of professional development, but given current gender roles, he is likely to have a different perspective about some of the issues that women face, as the Stanford data seem to indicate. This does not mean, of course, that all women are good mentors or that graduate students accept all women as equally valuable in their mentoring.[12]

Another area in which the sex of the mentor can make a difference is in sexual harassment. While same-sex sexual harassment exists, it is rare among women.[13] But the sexual harassment of female graduate students by male faculty members is all too common. Reports of sexual harassment in surveys range from 2 percent of female students in entomology who reported sexual blackmail to 18 percent of women who experienced faculty members making suggestive gestures or comments about their bodies or their sexuality to 25 percent of female psychology students in clinical training having sexual relations with their supervisors.[14] These figures are complemented by the admission by 25 percent of male faculty members surveyed in 1988 that they have had sex with students, generally more than once.[15]

Finally, there is some evidence that students collaborate more with same-sex mentors, collaboration being measured by publication of an article or writing a grant proposal, and establish closer professional relationships with same-sex faculty members. Women collaborate more than men in those fields (such as

Graduate Career Indices	Percentage Responding Always or Often			
	Men	Women	Chi²	Sample Size[1]
Creative				
How important is the following to your career choice:				
Intellectual challenge	99	99	4.53	624
Kind of people you work with	87	91	8.12	624
Opportunity to be creative	99	97	4.90	622
Chance to use skills	74	95	8.47*	621
Chance to take risks	45	33	14.36***	624
Chance to do seminal work	76	61	18.94***	622
Work Pressure				
How important is the following to your career choice:				
Little pressure and stress	26	23	4.97	618
Kind of people you work with	87	91	8.12	624
Flexible time schedule	67	77	18.29***	621

Source: Adapted from Zappert and Stansbury, Table IV.

*Indicates significance at 0.05.
**Indicates significance at 0.01.
***Indicates significance at 0.001.
[1]Sample size varies because of missing value.

Figure 4. *Importance of Creative Elements and Work Pressure to Graduate Career Choices.*

13

physics) where collaboration is not necessarily the norm:[16]

It does come down to which "c" word you choose, competition or cooperation. I certainly know some women who are very—apparently anyway—comfortable and seem to thrive on competition. But even those women, you sit and talk to them, and they'll say they'd rather be cooperative. The system is not set up that way, it's set up to be a competitive system (graduate student).

Graduate students, like their undergraduate counterparts in the previous section, find that "pervasive subtle discrimination can do as much damage as, if not more damage than, isolated incidents of overt discrimination." The types of subtle discrimination that have a negative impact on the experience of women graduate students in science, engineering and mathematics include:

◆ being treated as women first and as professionals second;

◆ being made invisible or being placed in a "fishbowl";

◆ patronizing behavior;

◆ questioning or discrediting of their qualifications;

◆ unwanted attention that at times became sexual or obscene; and

◆ advisers' behavior, including lack of support or presumption of failure, wariness about taking on graduate students with children, and devaluation of women's scientific contributions.[17]

The thing that seems to discourage women most at the graduate level is the sense of isolation within their departments. When students feel isolated, they do not get the level of professional and personal support that could make the difference

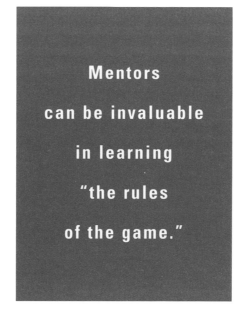

Mentors can be invaluable in learning "the rules of the game."

between success and failure. In the words of Wanda Patterson, an African American engineering Ph.D., "When there is no one to share your ideas and problems, you don't know that there are others studying as intensely as you are."[18] Given women's different motivations for choosing and staying in science careers, when faculty members ignore differences and treat all students the same, such treatment may translate into a sense among women students that they are not part of the research group or the department.

While top notch post-doc positions were available to me, there is a great shortage of faculty positions. Having made the commitment to stay in Austin with my family, I found none. My only option was a non-tenure track position on soft money.

—*woman research associate, natural sciences Ph.D.*[1]

For some time now a doctorate in science has not been the key to a tenure-line academic position, especially in doctoral-level universities. A post-doctoral position has become a required experience for those women and men whose ultimate goal is to become an academic scientist. Post-doctoral fellowships were meant to be an enriching year or two that allowed recent graduates to accumulate the additional publications and/or research experience needed to make them competitive for higher-level jobs. In a comparison of effects on productivity of post-doctoral positions, Grant and Ward report that female chemists had published somewhat less than male counterparts. However, the same was not true of sociologists and physicists.[2] But in today's job market, these positions are essential in a different way and have acquired a different function. Many post-doctoral fellowships have become low-paying, revolving holding pens for increasingly frustrated graduates who cannot find permanent positions.[3] At present, there is great variability in the rules that govern post-doctoral fellowships. Because the rules of the game for post-doctoral fellows are even more ambiguous than in graduate school, it is possible that women are less able to move beyond these types of positions. Furthermore, the official rules of the game can be different from institution to institution, or even from department to department.

With decreasing resources allocated to science and increasing numbers of doctorate-level individuals, it is now common to go from one post-doctoral position to another. And often, when a faculty position is found, it is a research position. In science, unlike other academic fields, there are relatively large numbers of faculty members in research positions. While significant in numbers, people in these positions do not wield much power since they are subject to the vagaries of funding:

> I found the constant pressure to stay funded too draining after ten years on soft money. Once, I had to let all of my technicians go and then retrain new ones. (woman research associate and natural sciences Ph.D)

While most available information is limited to faculty members in tenure-track positions, these numbers do not reflect the total presence of women as a whole in academic science. Using numbers for the University of Washington for 1990 (excluding the School of Medicine) as indicative of the situation at large public research institutions would lead to the conclusion that tenure-track faculty women are less than one-half of all faculty women. In 1990 women constituted 14 percent of all tenure-track faculty members but 34 percent of all faculty members, including 47 percent of researchers and 12 percent of lecturers. In the School of Medicine, women make up approximately 10 percent of tenure-track faculty members and 14 percent of all faculty members, but comprise 49 percent of non-tenured faculty members, 37 percent of research faculty members, 36 percent of residents and fellows, and 62 percent of non-faculty researchers.

Among the teaching ranks at the national level, in 1991 women in science and engineering fields represented "29 percent of the assistant professors, 21 percent of the associate professors, and 9 percent of the full professors."[4] Nonetheless, these numbers do reflect the percentage of women who are in the more secure and powerful positions in academia.

With numbers like these it should come as no surprise that Etzkowitz and his colleagues report that isolation is the major problem faced by women faculty members and women graduate students in science departments (physics, chemistry, biology,

> Those women who had networks, peer groups, or mentors were more likely to persevere than those women who were isolated.

computer science, and electrical engineering). Yet the mere presence of more women in the same department does not necessarily eliminate the sense of isolation.[5] Rank seems to make a difference in how people experience their environment. In a study of both science and non-science faculty members in the College of Sciences and Humanities at Ball State University, Kite and Balogh find that while women faculty members are more dissatisfied with their job situations than men, untenured women are the most dissatisfied. They also report that untenured women are significantly more dissatisfied with their relations with their colleagues than are their untenured male colleagues.[6]

Those women who had networks, peer groups, or mentors were more likely to persevere than those women who were isolated. The kind and the timing of support is important. As a study of Latina faculty members by Prieto-Dayard and her colleagues indicates, the support crucial to feeling satisfaction with an academic career is not personal support but support of professional issues—including validation of areas of research that are not seen as mainstream within the discipline and approval of funds for research in such areas.[7] Preston reports that those women who had mentors early in their careers were more likely to remain in science or engineering. A mentor can make all the difference, as the two quotes that follow illustrate:

I was only allowed to work in my previous position because of support from a senior member of the department who was five years from retirement. (woman research associate and natural sciences Ph.D.)
I have felt completely isolated since then. (a junior female faculty member who stopped working with her male mentor after he indicated that her having a child would have a negative impact on her tenure decision)[8]
The studies of women faculty members in science, mathematics, and engineering indicate clearly that in all measures of success, women lag behind men:

◆ women receive fewer promotions, even when controlling for productivity, years since doctorate, fields, and receipt of prestigious fellowships;

◆ women advance more slowly than men with data normalized for educational background, years of experience, and research productivity;

◆ studies in chemistry and in pharmacy show that women's salaries are lower than men's, although in psychology (where women constitute a significant proportion) they are almost equal; and

◆ women publish less than men, with differences varying by field.
The publication rate of women is not affected by marriage, and the reported effects of children are different in various studies, with most indicating a positive effect.[9] Preston notes that among men and women at comparable stages in their careers a similar proportion are married, but men are more likely to be employed

Biology professor Mary Dunn and student, Boston College

and to be parents.[10] As Mary Frank Fox notes, marriage and children may have no negative effects on those women who constitute the sample for those studies: those who are still in academia.[11]

In two studies examining the reasons for scientists leaving science, family caretaking responsibilities are a factor, although in one of the studies not the most important factor for leaving. In a follow-up study to her economic models of career change, using surveys of the career trajectories of fifteen hundred male and female natural science and engineering alumni, Anne Preston found that the majority of the women who left science report that need to care for family was a motivating factor in their decision. The caretaking responsibilities came in the form of married women taking on more of the household chores (65 percent while their spouses were responsible for only 35 percent), taking on more of the childcare (60 percent versus 15 percent), or altering their location to satisfy their spouse's career constraints (44 percent of women versus 23 percent of men).

In a further study of fifty-two women, one-half of whom had stayed in science or engineering and one-half of whom had left, Preston identified four factors contributing to the likelihood that a woman will leave a science career. *First,* the struggle to balance family life and the profession over time results in compromise of the career. For those with a Ph.D., this conflict often revolves around the difficulty of finding a geographical location where both members of the couple could work in their chosen careers. In contrast, women with a bachelor's or master's degree

employed in industry find the conflict between the needs of their children and the inflexible environment of the company more of a problem. *Second,* lack of mentoring early in the career may influence the choice to leave. Almost all of the women who stayed in science reported that they had

> **Household responsibilities and caretaking are not the top sources of stress for men or women. The top stressors are all job-related: time pressures, lack of personal time, and teaching load.**

encouragement and support of mentors, especially early in their careers. *Third,* many women feel that their interests are not well matched to the narrow focus of their jobs. *Finally,* these women report feeling frustrated that their behavior and performance are judged by more stringent stan-

dards than are applied to the men around them.[12]

In our study of thirty-nine scientists (thirty women and nine men) who left science after obtaining at least one job beyond the graduate degree, concern with caretaking responsibilities (for elderly parents as well as for children) was a reason given by women but not by men. Caretaking responsibilities, however, were not women's main reason for leaving. When asked to rank the reasons in order of importance, financial concerns (such as denied tenure and unavailability of grants) were ranked as most important by both women and men, followed by working conditions (tired of uncertainty or of long hours, sexual harassment);[13] the existence of other, better opportunities; and caretaking responsibilities for both children and other family members.[14] Thus, while among scientists in both studies caretaking responsibilities may be mostly a "women's issue," it is not identified as the most important factor in making decisions about leaving science by women in one of the studies. Similarly, in Eric Dey's recent study of stressors among faculty members, household responsibilities and caretaking are not the top sources of stress for either men or women (including both tenured and untenured and Whites and non-Whites). The top stressors are all job-related: time pressures, lack of personal time, and teaching load.[15]

The importance, but not the preeminence, of family responsibilities is also borne out in a study of the reasons given by women faculty members for leaving academic jobs at a prestigious liberal arts college where 9 percent of women and 2.5 percent of men left before tenure decision. Concerns about social and family life are listed among the top four reasons for leaving, but are not more important than barriers to conducting research, including unrealistic expectations from departments, heavy teaching demands, lack of support, and psychological factors such as stress.[16]

In an institutional analysis of eleven cohorts of tenure-track hires in a large public coeducational research university, the cumulative percentage of women who left before tenure was slightly higher than men (33.6 percent versus 31.6 percent), as was the percentage of women who were denied tenure compared to the percentage for men (10.3 percent of all women who went up for tenure versus 7 percent of all men). While favoring men, neither of these differences was significant. These numbers are not different from those reported for Preston's sample. Only 10 percent of those scientists with Ph.D.'s were working in unrelated occupations, and this did not differ by gender. Thus, apart from the issue of caretaking, where mixed results have been obtained by the few studies conducted so far, there seem to be more similarities than differences in the data available on women and men who leave academia or academic science.

It is among those who stay that we see disparities by field not only in the numbers of women, but also in the rewards that accompany success—awards, promotions, access to resources, salary, and more importantly, a sense of belonging and being taken seriously. The lack of such rewards takes its toll in terms of the women's sense of competence and

belonging: "I guess I've gotten more confident as I get older and take on more jobs like editor in chief of a journal and so on. I still notice feelings of lack of confidence and maybe I'm not good enough to do this."[17]

> Latina faculty members in the California state system reported that both racism and sexism affected them significantly.

Discrimination can be experienced in the form of racism or sexism. Latina faculty members in the California state system reported that both racism and sexism affected them significantly.[18] In Dey's report on stress factors for faculty members, subtle discrimination was mentioned as a great source of stress by faculty members of color, especially tenured faculty members. White women also find subtle discrimination stressful.[19]

In a 1991 survey of American Astronomical Society (AAS) members, 40 percent of the women but only 12 percent of the men reported that they experienced or witnessed discrimination against women. As the executive director of the society put it: "Things I don't think are offensive

are wildly offensive to my female colleagues."[20]

The culture of an institution and/or department can make a difference in rates of sexual harassment as Dey, Sax, and Korn have documented; among the SME fields the highest levels of sexual harassment are reported in agriculture and engineering (23.5 percent and 19.6 percent) and the lowest in mathematics and statistics (7.6 percent).[21] In a follow-up study of the AAS survey, Jill Price reports that female astronomers in academia (65 percent of the sample) are three times more likely to have said they were harassed than are those in private industry.[22] Regardless of the form or institutional setting, instances of discrimination were discouraging to women faculty members.

What we see, then, in all levels of academic science, is a consistent pattern. Even if they like and succeed at their work, many women scientists feel isolated or alienated from the ethos of competition that admits no other commitment beyond their scientific work. As one of the participants in the Oral History Project of the Northwest Center for Research on Women said:

> I'm sure I could still be a productive scientist and come up with interesting results and train good students, be a good teacher—just not at the hyper driving level everyone does it—and there should be room for people like that. I don't know why it has to be all or nothing. (woman physical sciences faculty member)

EXPLAINING WOMEN'S EXPERIENCES IN ACADEMIC SCIENCE

The culture on some campuses seemed to make it difficult to employ sociological or social-psychological explanations for the problems experienced by SME women. Theories of this order were sometimes dismissed, [not only by men but by the women themselves] as admissions of weakness; as an unwelcome justification for special treatment; or as [unacceptable] "feminist" thinking.

—Seymour and Hewitt, 383

Despite purportedly equal access, education, and career opportunities in science, mathematics, and engineering, there is plenty of evidence that the experiences of women and men are different in many crucial respects. The best explanations we have today to account for these different experiences are psycho-sociological explanations; these simultaneously take into account the socialization that women bring to academia and the discriminatory structure of academic science.

A model that may be used to explain individual women's sense of competence is Bandura's Perceived Self-Efficacy (one's sense of being able and capable).[1] In this model, an individual's perceived self-efficacy is determined by four sources of efficacy information:

◆ past experience of accomplishments;
◆ emotional arousal, often meaning freedom from anxiety;
◆ vicarious learning or modeling (especially from others like us); and
◆ verbal persuasion and support from others.

Using Bandura's model, one can explain how women who have equal or higher grades than men and who obtain equal or higher degrees still feel less accomplished and accepted and continue to judge their performance to be less than successful. If

they have no models from whom to learn and if they receive no verbal support from others, women's sense of self-efficacy can be diminished to the point where it negatively affects performance. As Seymour and Hewitt found, the individual coping skills that predicted persistence were hard work and ability, intrinsic interest in the discipline, and an independent sense of confidence in one's ability.[2]

Bandura's model and other explanatory concepts such as attribution theory can help us understand that portion of outcomes in performance which can be accounted for by the interaction of the individual with the environment.[3] In Bandura's model, there is only one factor that is

totally beyond the reach of the current institutional climate: past experience of accomplishments. Otherwise, the present institutional setting in which the individual finds her or himself affects the remaining three factors.

Academic institutions cannot change women's past experiences. They can, however, affect the learning opportunities through responsive measures to eliminate discriminatory external barriers that consistently give women the message that they do not belong in science. Individuals and groups in institutions can work to eliminate the chilly and discouraging climate for women in science, engineering, and mathematics.

Harvard University molecular biologist Lydia Villa-Komaroff

Each woman in SME has an investment in having a satisfying and productive experience in her field. An increasing number of men in the academic environment also see this as a task for the whole institution and not just for individual women in support of themselves. The recommendations that follow are divided into individual and institutional recommendations. The recommendations for institutions suggest concrete ways to support women undergraduate and graduate students, post-doctoral fellows, and faculty members in SME. The recommendations for individuals suggest how both women and men might take steps on behalf of women in SME fields. The recommendations are a distillation of those made by many researchers and are acknowledged when a source is known.

These recommendations are given in the spirit of the beginning allegory. While many of us have been trained to believe that fairness means treating everyone in the same way, we have discovered through practice that equality is not always achieved by treating everyone the same. In fact, equating sameness with equality sometimes creates even more pronounced inequities. When the plants were treated the same, many did not flourish. When only the strong ones were nourished, most plants died. Only with the caretaker who said, "I try to provide what each plant needs," did all the plants in the conservatory flourish. The challenge in higher education is to implement a more student-centered and complex notion of equality to insure that all

students thrive. In the words of Hall and Sandler, "women's educational experiences may differ considerably from those of men, even when they attend the same institutions, share the same classrooms, and work with the same graduate advisors."[1] Fairness, then, may be best served not by treating all students or faculty members in the same way, but by considering the diversity of needs and constructing an academic climate that is more likely to enhance each person's fulfillment of their promise.

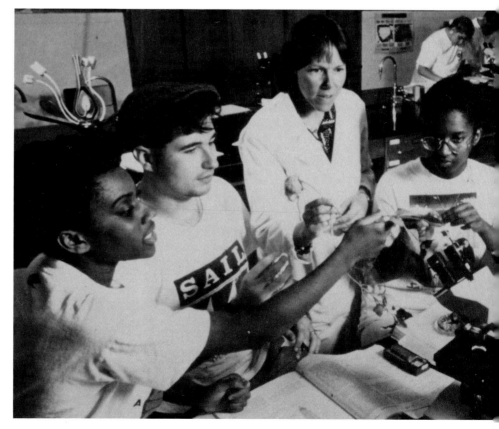

Rollins College

20

Some institutions have taken the lead in developing programs to address concerns of women in SME fields, as well as in supporting those individuals who are making a difference for women on their campus. Most of the interventions are still aimed at "enabling students and/or faculty members from underrepresented groups to fit into, adjust to, or negotiate the existing system."[1] A few institutions are taking the lead in focusing on the culture of the institution or the department so that women as well as men are given the flexibility to strive for excellence using a variety of approaches. These institutions are recognizing that women bring with them styles of learning and working that enrich science. They are also recognizing what Tobias has been assert-

ing since the publication of *They're Not Dumb, They're Different*: many male students benefit from the changes that were assumed would be beneficial only to women and or ethnic minorities.[2]

A program, for example, that focuses on how faculty members can make their classrooms and departments more woman-friendly and inclusive has been initiated at Brown University. Funded by the Sloan Foundation, the first phase of this program consists of visits during regular departmental meetings to discuss issues women face, followed by faculty seminars. A third phase is about to begin, with a small group of faculty members working directly on curricular change and course modification.[3]

Many universities have special programs either across the university or in a particular discipline to encourage women students to participate in science fields. Components of these recruitment and retention programs include: summer outreach or transitions programs, curriculum development and single-sex classroom experiences, mentoring, and various levels of professional and social support, such as residence halls for women in non-traditional fields, peer study, and counseling groups. As Rosser and Davis demonstrate in their forthcoming review of current programs, the effectiveness of many programs has yet to be evaluated. But programs at Cornell University, Dartmouth University, Rutgers University, Mills College, Oberlin College, Purdue University, the University of California–Davis, the University of Maryland, and the University of

Washington have been evaluated and found to have positive effects on the retention of women in science, engineering, and mathematics.[4] The Women in Engineering Program Advocates Network (WEPAN) is conducting a national evaluation of all existing Women in Engineering programs.

As Matyas and Malcolm propose in their overview of the "future of intervention" programs, the aim must be an integrated model of science education. In this model, isolated projects ought to lead logically to departmental or school-based efforts, which in turn lead to increased levels of coordination of discrete programs that culminate in structural reform. This path of development moves from individual commitments to institutional ones.[5] The recommendations below work best where, like in the Matyas and Malcolm model of intervention, there are people at all levels in the system who support the conscious actions by faculty members and students to break the negative cycle of differences in experiences for all women.[6]

RECOMMENDATIONS FOR CHANGE

For Undergraduate Students—In the Classroom

◆ *In class discussion, give credit to women.* If the point you are making follows from or reinforces a point previously made by a woman, mention that in your statement: "As Terry was saying before…" makes Terry's contribution visible.

◆ *Let go of any tendencies to be self-critical and of the fear of being wrong.*[1] Ask questions. You are paying for being taught what you do not know. A professor or teaching assistant who criticizes questions is not fulfilling his or her duty. If asked a question for which you are not sure of the answer, venture your best guess—your hunch may be as good as any other student's.

◆ *Be assertive and persist in asking faculty members for what you need.*[2] Do not apologize for asking for what you need; you can be thankful when you get it.

◆ *Give positive feedback to your professors for efforts to create an equitable climate.* You can do this during class through nods and other responsive cues, during office hours by stating how you appreciate the specific behavior, and through student evaluations.

◆ *Use your student evaluation form to comment on climate issues in the classroom.* Describe both the positive and the negative and provide context for your statements. To say that the teacher is not responsive to students' concerns is not as informative as saying that the teacher did not respond to reports of harassing behavior by students.

◆ *Observe behaviors in the classroom and in the lab.* If you notice patterns of discrimination, call these to the attention of the teaching assistant, lab assistant, or professor. Some patterns that may be observed include: men always using equipment first, women assigned to the role of assistant, and women being consistently interrupted. If there is no response from your immediate instructor, discuss your concerns with an advisor and/or with people at the campus-based program or professional organization you belong to.

For Undergraduate Students—Everywhere

◆ *Learn to be open and direct but tactful.* This has been characterized as a male style of communication, but it is really the result of an independent and self-efficacious sense of self.

◆ *Do not take criticism personally.*[3] Even if the criticism is stated personally, do not translate the hurt or discouragement into, "The professor dislikes me, therefore it's no use to try," or, "This is the end of my career in this major."

◆ *Bond to other people in your major and study in groups.*[4] Treisman has pointed out that studying in groups improved the performance of students in mathematics.[5] Chacón et al. reported that students who kept in contact with at least two other students through the school year were more likely to finish on time and have better grades than did students who did not have such support.[6]

◆ *Participate in campus-based programs.* Programs such as Women in Engineering, Women in Science, or Minorities in Science and Engineering Program provide skills, support, and information. Student clubs and honorary societies provide ways of finding individuals with common interests that can offer support.

◆ *Join women's professional societies.* If your college does not have a campus-based program, the Association for Women in Science or the Society of Women Engineers may have a chapter in your community or region. These organizations will be useful for finding summer jobs, networking and resume writing, and as a source of practical information.[7]

◆ *Be familiar with grievance procedures.* Undergraduates are the least likely members of the academic community to use grievance procedures, but every campus has someone, such as an ombudsman or someone in the Office of Student Affairs, who is assigned to hear grievances from students. Some campuses allow for confidential complaints to be made. In addition, on some campuses the women's center can help with complaints.

◆ *If you have a choice try to get on-campus jobs, preferably in labs or other SME-related sites.*[8] SME-related jobs will allow not only for a direct experience that can affirm the SME major but will also give access to potential mentors and role models. If you are thinking of going to graduate school, and you have not had time for extra-curricular activities, an SME-related job experience will enhance your opportunities for admission.

◆ *In choosing graduate school or jobs, take climate issues into consideration.* In choosing graduate schools to apply to, find out how many women students and faculty members are at these schools. Check also for the existence of any programs targeted for women. Fay Ajzenberg-Selove, in her *A Matter of Choices: Memoirs of a Female Physicist,* says, "I would recommend to young women that they do not accept admissions to graduate departments which do not have at least a couple of women faculty members, preferably tenured, and several women graduate students....A woman is less likely to make it if these supports do not exist."[9]

For Graduate Students

◆ *Practice the fine art of externalizing; don't let negatives get you down.* Ask yourself: "Is this a situational issue? Does this happen to every student or to every woman I know?" Even if you think that a bad grade or evaluation was your fault, can you say to yourself, "I was having a bad day" rather than, "I'm no good at this?" Clewell and Ginorio discuss how an awareness of discrimination, be it racism or sexism, is positively related to persistence. (See "Explaining Women's Experiences in Academic Science," note 3, for a reason why women may have a hard time doing this.)

◆ *Don't discount your own experiences.* If a bad feeling persists, pay attention to it. Compare notes with your classmates or with your colleagues in other departments. For example, if you feel like you and/or women are being ignored in a seminar or class, or that a particular individual hogs the discussion, there are probably others who feel the same. Even if you decide to do nothing about the situation, knowing that you are not the only one feeling like this will make you feel better.

◆ *Recognize your own styles and learn how to keep the balance between the departmental climate, your advisor's style and your own style.* As Etzkowitz et al. state, "In graduate school, behavior is expected to be independent, strategic and void of interpersonal support. These expectations are antithetical to traditional female socialization."[10] Find support elsewhere if necessary.

◆ *Pick good role models and mentors and widen the circle beyond the department if necessary.* Women want role models "who [can] concretely explain the necessary strategies and steps to be taken to succeed in graduate school."[11] If there are only one or two women professors in your department, you may not find them congenial to your style or your needs. Do not feel limited to them or disloyal if you go to others for mentoring.

◆ *Select advisors carefully.*[12] Change advisors if necessary. In selecting advisors, pay attention to the political realities of your department as well as the scientific expertise of your advisors. If you are caught in the middle of some conflict, consider changing advisors.

◆ *Be aware of the future consequences of career-related decisions.* Widnall emphasizes the importance of seeing the continuity of your experiences as a graduate student with your future career.[13] Every decision you make as a graduate student can have long-term and unintended consequences. For example, if you love teaching and limit your experiences as a graduate student to teaching, you will not have the breadth of experience that will make you competitive once you graduate.

◆ *Belong to active networks of peers as well as professional groups.*[14] If there are enough interested women, form a student group. It can be an informal group that meets once a week for coffee and talk or a formal group that will provide access to student or departmental funds to sponsor speakers, receptions, etc. If you are one of few women, and men are not welcoming in your department, find colleagues in your field through e-mail networks or by attending professional conferences.[15]

Faculty Members—In Support of Themselves or Other Faculty

◆ *Do not expect more of your female colleagues in terms of support than you do of male colleagues.* Expect support from your colleagues in proportion to your investment in the department, the closeness of your field of work to theirs, or based on their personality, but not based on their gender. Do not judge more harshly female colleagues who are not supportive than you do your unsupportive male colleagues.

◆ *Learn how to mentor your colleagues.* Mentoring is a complex interaction that, poorly done, can be experienced as patronizing and/or thoughtless. Provide at least five types of support: cueing the newcomer to risks, passing on informal as well as formal knowledge, giving feedback on both personal and professional role performance, modeling the standards to be followed, and empathizing with and encouraging junior colleagues.[16]

◆ *Say "no" when you need to and do not feel guilty about it.* If you are one of the a women in your department or college, you will be asked by colleagues and students to do many activities or serve in many committees. Say "no" as often as you need to, especially if you are trying to get tenure or if your position is supported by research monies. If you are concerned about not being a good citizen, note how many committees or service activities your male colleagues at the same level do. When you are asked to serve, ask how this service will be evaluated. If this information is not in agreement with the written information that you have been given, seek more information from other sources.

◆ *Learn exactly what is expected of you in order to gain tenure, be promoted, or* ⸻ *any other kinds of rewards.* Ask your chair, or any other individuals charged with the ultimate decision about these issues in your department, how your work will be evaluated. If possible, get that statement in writing. Ask for as many operational details as you would need if you were running an experiment. Ask your mentors what questions you need to ask in order to get a clear answer and what cues you have to watch for in order to understand the implications of that answer. Get personally acquainted with every voting member in your department and make appointments to see them if necessary. Ensure that they are familiar with the significance of your work. In the words of Carol Eastman, senior vice president and executive vice chancellor, University of Hawaii–Manoa, "When you are going up for tenure, you need to understand how to behave with the authority tenure bestows upon you, you have to—in a sense—act as if you are tenured already to be seen as 'worthy.'"[17]

◆ *Support flexibility in the system, including tenure.* Do not automatically oppose any changes to the system or tenure, promotion, and other rewards for productivity. Do not assume that changes in the rigidity of the tenure system with regard to time to tenure will result in diminished productivity or commitment that will affect the quality of the department.

◆ *Develop collaborative working relations both in and out of your department.* If these are not possible, become a part of a professional network. These collaborations will make your work visible to others and will provide opportunities for gaining informal knowledge. They may also provide opportunities for gaining personal support. Think of people in industry as possible collaborators.[18]

◆ *Participate in the activities of the women's caucus of your professional organization.* Even if you are not active in the caucus, responding to the surveys which are used for monitoring at the national level will provide the kind of information (such as national averages of salaries) that can be useful to you when negotiating promotions.

Faculty Members—In Support of Students

◆ *Change the philosophy and structure of pedagogy and grading to reward different kinds of learning.*[19] In addition to individual work and assessments, incorporate activities that also allow for group work. In forming groups, be aware of the dynamics of the groupings in terms of gender, ethnicity, and working styles—a poorly-formed group is as discouraging as a very competitive classroom.[20]

◆ *Include women's work in your course.* This is especially important in introductory survey courses. Mention women scientists' names so that it is obvious that women have been contributors.

◆ *Check the textbooks you use for non-stereotypical inclusion of women.* Including women and trivializing their contributions is worse than not including women at all. A widely-used plant ecology textbook, for example, makes the following reference to the wife of a famous botanist: "It is clear that she was a great help to him in his career, functioning alternatively as driver, secretary, photographer, translator, and sometimes co-author."[21] Inform the publisher's representative of why you are not selecting the book. Put it in writing.

◆ *Check your own behaviors that might create a chilly climate for women.* The list offered in *The Classroom Climate: A Chilly One for Women?*[22] is a useful place to look for specific behaviors, such as making seemingly helpful comments which imply that women are not as competent as men: "I know women usually have trouble with numbers, but I'll be glad to give you extra help."

◆ *Keep in mind students' lives beyond the department.* Do not schedule course activity so that seventy or more hours per week are needed in order to fulfill requirements. Many students have family responsibilities, and many others need to have outside jobs in order to pay for their expenses.[23]

◆ *Try more than one approach.* No single measure can solve all concerns. Much depends on the students, the institutional climate, and your own style. If an approach works for someone else it may not work for you and vice-versa.

◆ *Encourage young women to discover the legacy that feminism has bequeathed to them and support them in being "assertive, active, and feminist."*[24] Encourage your students to read the books listed in the annotated bibliography and recommend that they read the biographies and autobiographies of women scientists. An updated list is available on request via Internet from nwcrow@u.washington.edu.

◆ *Ensure that the classroom behavior of students is not discouraging or disparaging to other students.* This must be done in a way that does not stigmatize women. The balancing of classroom dynamics is facilitated by setting a tone from the beginning of classes about appropriate behavior towards anyone and then calling attention to the deviations which occur—including those directed against women. While it may not be possible to catch every instance as it occurs, do not automatically dismiss as oversensitivity reports that women students make to you or your assistants.

◆ *Reward your colleagues who do mentoring or who change their behavior as described above and point out unacceptable behavior.* If you are a junior professor, you may be limited in the range of ways in which you can do this without risk. If you are a senior professor, you can offer advice when necessary, and ensure that these concerns are taken seriously by including them among factors to be considered for promotion, tenure, salary increases, and other rewards in your department.

◆ *Instead of adapting women to existing structures, negotiate for changes in courses and institutional policies.*[25] Unlike many of the proposals above, this requires convincing others in your department to work with you. Begin by using informal occasions to lobby your colleagues and use faculty meetings and other official opportunities to bring up the issue. Circulate supportive materials. In academic institutions, change initiated from the bottom can take two to three years for approval because of the procedures required for approval.

Administrators—Chairs and Above

◆ *Support programs for women and other underrepresented student groups.* This support can range from inviting representatives of such programs to make presentations at one of the faculty meetings to making financial contributions to the programs. Become an institutional member of a women's organization (see the list of organizations in the "Resources" section).

◆ *Develop admissions policies that do not put undue weight on the GRE and other timed measures of achievement.* You may consider adjusting admissions formulas that include timed measures of achievement for their underprediction of women's success in college.[26]

◆ *Recruit students in groups.* Wanda Patterson, a Ph.D. in engineering, suggests, "Send students to graduate school in threes; then you will get graduates."[27] A built-in support system increases the probability of success for any underrepresented student.

◆ *Assure equal access to resources (lab equipment, computers, RAs, travel), teaching loads, interaction.* Allocating equitably from among those that apply is not enough. Insuring that women have the information that these resources are available for allocation is an important component in increasing the likelihood that they will apply.[28]

◆ *Increase the number of students, teaching assistants, and faculty members who are women.* Keep as a goal to increase these numbers until they reflect the availability pool.[29]

◆ *Increase women's visibility.* Ensure that the colloquium committee invites women speakers. Support women's requests for travel to conferences where they will be making presentations. Submit their names when nominations are requested for awards and other opportunities.

◆ *Monitor outcomes.* Do so not only cross-sectionally but also longitudinally. Evidence of an increase in numbers of women students or faculty members from year to year is not an indicator of success if, due to a revolving door, these numbers represent different individuals.

RECOMMENDATIONS FOR CHANGE

- *Clearly outline the expectations for junior faculty members.* Provide these expectations in writing, offer guidance in implementation, and review periodically with the faculty member so that corrective action can be taken.[30]
- *Provide each junior faculty member with a mentoring committee.* This committee could provide the following types of support: cueing the newcomer to risks, passing on informal as well as formal knowledge, helping to set realistic goals, giving feedback on both personal and professional role performance, and empathizing with and encouraging junior colleagues.[31]
- *Support women faculty members in your department, division, or program.* This is especially important when they are the only one or one of a handful of women. Be attentive to ways they might come more fully into their own as academic scientists if their environment encouraged their growth. Consider leadership opportunities for your female colleagues; point out opportunities they might not know about that might enhance their scholarship.
- *Monitor that the women in your department, division, or program are not overextended to the detriment of their professional careers.* Many women, especially if there are very few or them, might assume undue responsibilities as mentors to women students in their field or be assigned an unusually high number of committee assignments. In addition, there is a pattern among many academic women to devote many out-of-class hours to student and institutional needs, sometimes at a high cost to their own professional advancement. Insure a balance for women's workload by allocating these duties to men, too, as well as by properly rewarding those who engage in it.

Administrators—Deans and Above

- *Assure students' safety.* Safety on campus, especially for women students doing lab work late at night, should be a high priority of the institution.[32]
- *Provide incentives for the creation of on-campus jobs in SME-related settings.* Ensure that women would have equal access to those jobs. If these jobs are open to work-study students, consider creating a pool of money to match off-campus salaries—often students will accept non-SME off-campus jobs because they are higher paying than on-campus jobs.
- *Do a self-study.* Look at your own record and make note of departments that are succeeding in keeping, graduating, and/or promoting women in SME.
- *Change the reward system.* As Linda Wilson said in February 1993 address to the AAAS, "Are we satisfied with the way we have structured our reward system to achieve excellence? Consider the following: We reward achievement in work without reference to the way work is balanced with other life responsibilities."[33] And, we may add, not much credit is given to excellence in teaching or advising.
- *Reward departments, colleges, and schools that do well.* Once your criteria for success have been set, reward those departments that meet or exceed those criteria.
- *Make department chairs and deans accountable.* Evaluate departments or schools on how effective they are in ensuring success with all students and faculty members. In departmental evaluations, ensure that activities that support women and other underrepresented students and faculty members are counted. Ensure that the chairs, in turn, include similar evidence in promotion and tenure decisions of their faculty members.[34]
- *Make your change efforts widely known.*[35] The visibility given to change activities legitimizes the efforts of all individuals below your level who are working toward a better climate. In settings where the top leadership makes it clear that improving the climate for women is a priority, there is a higher degree of participation.[36]
- *Tailor your programs to the needs of different groups on campus.* In Dey's words: "Rather than taking a 'one size fits all' approach, institutions should pay attention to the stressors that affect different groups of faculty."[37]
- *Revise the tenure process.* Ensure that "every tenure-review committee has at least one female member,"[38] that the application of tenure rules is not inflexible, and that it does not penalize women or men who take advantage of opportunities such as "stop-the-tenure clock" for caretaking responsibilities.
- *Support or establish an Office on the Status of Women Faculty Members.* This office should be chaired by a senior professor reporting directly to the chief administrative officer of the campus.[39]

Scientific and Professional Organizations

◆ *Assure women's participation at all levels of official activities.* From insuring that women are not excluded from being invited as speakers in the regional and national conventions to equitably distributing travel funds to graduate students, make sure that women are visible in your organization.[40] Make sure that women are seriously considered for positions of power, such as journal editor.

◆ *Establish and/or support the women's caucus of your organization.* Women's caucuses in the various professional organizations have been responsible for documenting and identifying ways of improving the status of women in the professions.[41]

◆ *Do periodic reports on the status of women in your organization.* Include an addendum that deals with gender issues to the surveys of salaries and other issues done by the organization. Make sure that data for the surveys is coded for demographic characteristics that are useful in monitoring the elimination of discrimination. Do not publish reports that do not break data by gender.

Introduction

1. As with all allegories there are quite a few assumptions built into this fable: 1) because the plants were not indigenous to the conservatory, the conservatory/academia is a "foreign" climate; 2) the plants are not passive; they are active in ways which are not understood by casual observers; and 3) the collector and most of the caretakers care about the plants.

2. The dropout rate for White students prevalent in many engineering schools even today ranges from 4 percent to about 74 percent, while the minority dropout rate ranges from 0 percent to about 98 percent, with a national average minority dropout rate in engineering at 38.7 percent (data from the National Action Council for Minorities in Engineering).

3. The climate of science has been hostile to lesbians and gays, too. Because lesbians and gays are not protected by federal regulations, however, information is not collected about any aspect of their experience on a national level. There are small studies that are starting to provide information about this population in some areas of science education. See Toni Clewell and Angela B. Ginorio, "Diverse Populations of Women and Girls in Science, Mathematics and Engineering" (paper for the CURIES Conference on Women in Science, Mathematics and Engineering, Wellesley, Mass., May 1994).

Climate as a Defining Issue

1. Elaine Seymour and Nancy M. Hewitt, *Talking About Leaving: Factors Contributing to High Attrition Rates Among Science, Mathematics and Engineering Undergraduate Majors,* final report to the Alfred P. Sloan Foundation on an ethnographic inquiry at seven institutions (Boulder, Colo.: University of Colorado Ethnography and Assessment Research and Bureau of Sociological Research, 1994); Susan Frazier-Kouassi et al., *Women in Mathematics and Physics: Inhibitors and Enhancers* (Ann Arbor: University of Michigan Center for the Education of Women, Department of Mathematics, and Department of Physics, 1992).

2. Henry Etzkowitz et al., "Athena Unbound: Barriers to Women in Academic Science and Engineering," *Science and Public Policy* (June 1992): 157–179; Henry Etzkowitz et al., "The Paradox of 'Critical Mass' for Women in Science," *Science* 266 (1994): 51–54.

3. Linda Grant and Kathyrn B. Ward, *Mentoring, Gender, and Publication Among Social, Natural and Physical Scientists* (Washington, D.C.: U.S. Department of Education, Office of Educational Research and Improvement, 1992).

4. Karen D. Arnold, "Undergraduate Aspirations and Career Outcomes of Academically Talented Women: A Discriminant Analysis," *Roeper Review* (February/March 1993): 170; L. T. Zappert and K. Stansbury, "In the Pipeline: A Comparative Analysis of Men and Women in Graduate Programs in Science, Engineering and Medicine at Stanford University," working paper, Stanford University Institute for Research on Gender, Stanford, Cal., 1987; Mary Frank Fox, "Women, Academia, and Careers in Science and Engineering" (paper for the CURIES Conference on Women in Science, Mathematics, and Engineering, Wellesley, Mass., May 1994).

Women in Scientific Fields

1. Betty M. Vetter, "Women in Science, Mathematics and Engineering: Myths and Realities" (paper for the CURIES Conference on Women in Science, Mathematics and Engineering, Wellesley, Mass., May 1994), 12; Carol Hollenshead et al., "Influences on Women Graduate Students in Engineering and Sciences: Rethinking a Gendered Institution" (paper for the CURIES Conferences on Women in Science, Mathematics and Engineering, Wellesley, Mass., May 1994), 5.

2. Marcia C. Linn, "Gender, Mathematics and Science: Trends and Recommendations" (paper for the Summer Institute for the Council of Chief State School Officers, June 1990), 26.

3. Vetter, 8.

4. Data sorted by the National Research Council at the request of the Northwest Center for Research on Women.

5. Fox, Table 3; Mildred Dresselhaus, "Update on the Chilly Climate for Women in Physics," *CSWP Gazette: Newsletter of the Committee on the Status of Women in Physics, American Physical Society* 14, no. 1 (1994): 4–9, 24; Helen Astin and Linda Sax, "College Women in Science: Personal and Environmental Influences on the Development of Scientific Talent" (paper for the CURIES Conference on Women in Science, Mathematics and Engineering, Wellesley, Mass., May 1994), Tables 3 and 4.

6. Fox, Table 4; Dresselhaus.

7. Nina Roscher, *Women Chemists 1990* (Washington, D.C.: Americal Chemical Society, 1990), 72–3.

8. Vetter, 25.

9. J. M. Gilligan, posting to Young Scientists Network Digest (#1190) e-mail list, 2 March 1993.

10. Mildred S. Dresselhaus, Judy R. Franz, and Bunny C. Clark, "Interventions to Increase the Participation of Women in Physics," *Science* 263, no. 5152 (1994): 1392.

11. Sylvia T. Bozeman, "Black Women Mathematicians: In Short Supply," *Sage* 6, no. 2 (1989): 19. In 1949 the two first Ph.D. degrees were granted by the University of Michigan to Marjorie Lee Brown and by Yale University to Evelyn Boyd Granville.

Entry Points for Women in Science

1. American Association of University Women, *How Schools Shortchange Girls* (report from AAUW, 1992), 1–117; Frazier-Kouassi et al.; Jane Butler Kahle, "The Schooling of Girls: Optimizing Opportunities or Obstacles?" (paper presented at the CURIES Conference on Women in Science, Mathematics and Engineering, Wellesley, Mass. May 1994).

2. Elizabeth Fennema, "Justice, Equity and Mathematics Education," in *Mathematics and Gender,* ed. E. Fennema and G. C. Leder (New York: Teachers College Press, 1990), 1–9.

3. Valerie E. Lee, Helen M. Marks, and Tina Byrd, "Sexism in Single-sex and Coeducational Secondary School Classrooms," *Sociology of Education* 67 (1994): 92–120.

4. Kahle, 21. Comparisons were done with African-American boys and girls, Asian-American boys and girls, and Latinos and Latinas.

5. J. R. Grignon, "Computer Experience of Menominee Indian Students: Gender Differences in Coursework and Use of Software," *Journal of American Indian Education* 32, no. 3 (1993): 1–15.

6. Measured by the NEAP proficiency scores for math and science.

7. Bailey in AAUW, 25–26.

8. Janet S. Hyde, Elizabeth Fennema, and Susan J. Lamon, "Gender Differences in Mathematics Performance: A Metanalysis," *Psychological Bulletin* 107, no. 2 (1990): 139–155.

9. J. S. Hyde, E. Fennema, M. Ryan, L. Frost, and C. Hopp, "Gender Comparisons of Mathematics Attitude and Affect," *Psychology of Women Quarterly* 14 (1990): 299–324.

10. Kahle.

11. A. Christopher Strenta et al.'s *Choosing and Leaving Science in Highly Selective Institutions,* final report to the Alfred P. Sloan Foundation (1993) suggests that pre-college preparation, especially in mathematics, is a major deciding factor in which students remain in SME majors.

12. Marcia C. Linn and Janet S. Hyde, "Gender, Mathematics, and Science," *Educational Researcher* 18, no. 9 (1989): 17–19, 22–27.

13. Strenta et al.

14. N. C. Ware, N. A. Steckler, and J. Lesserman, "Undergraduate Women: Who Chooses a Science Major?, *Journal of Higher Education* 56, no. 1 (1988): 73–84; C. Ethington, "Differences Among Women Intending to Major in Quantitative Fields of Study," *Journal of Educational Research* 81, no. 6 (1988): 354–59.

15. Seymour and Hewitt, 312–13.

16. Colleges themselves may encourage stereotypical expectations. In the fall 1994 issue of the Yale University *Parents' Newsletter,* a young woman is quoted approvingly in the article "Perspectives from the Class of 1998": "You mean I can take classes in Chinese poetry or child psychology? And I can avoid math completely? What a school!" (5).

The Undergraduate Experience

1. Angela B. Ginorio et al., *Patterns of Persistence: Switching and Attrition Among Science and Engineering Majors for Women and Men Students at the University of Washington, 1985–1991* (final report to the Alfred P. Sloan Foundation, July 1994). In this sample it was found that women were more willing to leave the physical sciences and forestry for the life sciences or other sciences.

2. Suzanne G. Brainard, personal communication with the author, 5 December 1994.

3. Sheila Humphreys and Robert Freeland, *Retention in Engineering: A Study of Freshman Cohorts,* report to the University of California Board of Regents (1992).

4. Strenta et al.

5. Pseudo-cohorts compare the numbers in the freshman class of a given year with the senior class four or five years later. This analysis assumes that all students enter and progress as the same rate, thus making the two populations the same. But in large public institutions students do not move through their education at an even pace. At the University of Washington, of an incoming class of 3,499 first-time freshmen, only 31.15 percent graduated in four years, suggesting that few students of the original cohort remain together in year four. Data covering 1981–1991 suggest that about 85 to 90 percent of students entering the university from high schools remain together between the first and second quarters of their first year.

6. Paula Rayman and Belle Brett, *Pathways for Women in the Sciences* (Wellesley, Mass: Wellesley College Center for Research on Women, 1993), 68–72.

7. Seymour and Hewitt, Table 12 and Table 13.

8. Suzanne G. Brainard, *The Freshman Intervention Program,* final report to the Alfred P. Sloan Foundation (Seattle: University of Washington, 1994), Table 5.

9. Seymour and Hewitt, 448.

10. Brainard, *The Freshman Intervention Program.*

11. Debbie Wiegand, Angela B. Ginorio, and Marsha D. Brown, *First Steps in College Science: A Comparison of Single-Sex versus Coeducational Programs,* final report to the Women's Colleges Coalition (October 1994).

12. Seymour and Hewitt, 448.

13. Astin and Sax.

14. Seymour and Hewitt, 309.

15. Karen D. Arnold, "Academically Talented Women in the 1980's: The Illinois Valedictorian Project," in *Women's Lives Through Time,* ed. K. D. Hulbert and D. T. Schuster (San Francisco: Jossey-Bass, 1993), 393–414. This is the study quoted by Widnall in her 1988 presidential lecture to AAAS, "Voices from the Pipeline." Whenever I have mentioned this study in the context of discussing issues for women in science to audiences composed mostly of women scientists or women graduate students in science, their reaction has been one of intense interest about these women. Their comments indicate that the paradox of low self-esteem in the face of high performance is familiar to them.

16. Arnold, "Undergraduate Aspirations," 170.

17. Arnold, "Academically Talented Women," 398.

18. Brainard, *The Freshman Intervention Program;* Seymour and Hewitt.

19. Astin and Sax, 11–12.

20. J. D. Davis, *The Effect of Mathematics Course Enrollment on Racial/Ethnic Differences in Secondary School Mathematics Achievement* (Princeton, N.J.: Educational Testing Service, 1986). When requesting this report ask for NAEP Report 86-EMC.

21. Jo Schnellman and Judith L. Gibbons, "Microinequities in the Classroom: The Perception by Minorities and Women of a Less Favorable Climate in the Classroom" (paper presented at the Annual Convention of the American Psychological Association, Toronto, Ont., August 1984).

22. Seymour and Hewitt, 328.

23. Louise F. Fitzgerald, "Sex and Denial in Scholarly Garb: The Special Case of Women in Science" (paper presented at the annual meeting of the American Association for the Advancement of Science, 1994); Marsha Brown and Angela B. Ginorio, "Female Bonding

as a Solution to Sexual Harassment Among Students" (paper for the Association for Women in Psychology Annual Conference, Seattle, Wash., February 1983).

24. Seymour and Hewitt, 351.

The Graduate Experience

1. Any other quotes identified only by the role of the speaker are part of the Northwest Center for Research on Women's Oral History Project or Career Change Project.

2. Female graduate students and research staff in the Laboratory for Computer Science and Artificial Intelligence Laboratory at MIT, *Barriers to Equality in Academia: Women in Computer Science at MIT* (Cambridge, Mass.: self-published, 1983), 1.

3. Hollenshead et al.

4. Rebecca Zwick, *Differences in Graduate School Attainment Patterns across Academic Programs and Demographic Groups,* research report of the Minority Education Project (Princeton, N.J.: Educational Testing Service, 1991), 11.

5. Preston.

6. Zwick, 2,13.

7. W. G. Bowen and N. L. Rudenstine, *In Pursuit of the Ph.D.* (Princeton, N.J.: Princeton University Press, 1992), 125–26.

8. David Redman (unpublished internal report, Princeton University, Princeton, N.J., 1994), 1–2; Osborne defines critical mass as "as strong minority of at least 15 percent."

9. Zappert and Stansbury.

10. Helen M. Berg and Marianne A. Ferber, "Men and Women Graduate Students: Who Succeeds and Why?" *Journal of Higher Education* 54, no. 6 (1983): 629–648.

11. G. A. Pearson "Gender, Race, Nationality, and the Graduate Student Entomology Experience," *American Entomologist* 38, no. 2 (1992):103–114.

12. Etzkowitz et al., "Athena Unbound," 172.

13. Peggy Stockdale, posting to SASH e-mail list, July 2, 1994.

14. Pearson, 108; J. Manis et al., *A Survey of the Graduate Experience: Sources of Satisfaction and Dissatisfaction Among Graduate Students at the University of Michigan* (Ann Arbor, Mich.: University of Michigan Center for the Education of Women, 1993), cited in Hollenshead et al., 14; Kevin Pope, Hanna Levenson, and Leslie R. Schover, "Sexual Intimacy in Psychology Training: Results and Implications of a National Survey," *American Psychologist* 34, no. 8 (1979): 68–9.

15. Louise F. Fitzgerald et al, "Academic Harassment: Sex and Denial in Scholarly Garb," *Psychology of Women Quarterly* 12, no. 3 (1988): 329–340. There are two schools of thought regarding the issue of sex between faculty members and students: those who argue that sex among consenting adults is fine as long as there is no coercion and no direct supervision of the student involved, and those who argue that sex between faculty members and students poses ethical and pragmatic problems (such as conflict of interest) that should be avoided at all cost. Schools across the country are amending their codes of conduct to reflect their positions.

16. Grant and Ward, 21; Berg and Ferber.

17. Female graduate students and research staff in the Laboratory for Computer Science and Artificial Intelligence Laboratory at MIT, 1–10; Etzkowitz et al., "Athena Unbound," 165–9.

18. Bozeman, 20.

The Faculty Experience

1. A. B. Ginorio, N. Barnett, and J. Keefer, *Survey of Career Change for Scientists* (in preparation).

2. Grant and Ward, 29–30.

3. The Young Scientists Network, an e-mail network, was formed to address these concerns. This group has been successful in bringing the concerns of unemployed or underemployed scientists to the attention of the scientific establishment, and recently to the public *(Newsweek,* 5 December 1994, 62).

4. Fox, Table 5.

5. Etzkowitz et al., "Paradox of 'Critical Mass,'" 6.

6. Mary Kite and Deb Balogh, "The Chilly Climate for Women Faculty" (paper presented at the Women and Gender Studies Lecture Series, Muncie, Ind., 1991), 10.

7. Mary Prieto-Dayard et al., "Environmental and Personal Characteristics Related to the Experience of Latinas in Academia," in *Sex Roles* (forthcoming).

8. Etzkowitz et al., "Gender Implosion: The Paradox of 'Critical Mass' for Women in Science" (manuscript, 1994), 6. See note 2 in "Climate as a Defining Issue."

9. Jonathan Cole, *Fair Science: Women in the Scientific Community* (New York: Free Press, 1979); Gerhardt Sonnert, "Careers of Women and Men Postdoctoral Fellows in Science," (paper presented at meetings of the American Sociological Association, August 1990); "On Target,"quoted in Young Scientists' Network e-mail network, 2. The study in chemistry did not control for other factors; the one in pharmacy did. As Fox makes clear, most contributions to publications are made by a few people—male or female, with the majority publishing very little (Fox, 9–10, 14).

10. Preston.

11. Fox.

12. These were a subset of the original sample of science and engineering alumnae (Preston).

13. Sexual harassment was mentioned only by women.

14. Ginorio et al., *Survey of Career Change.*

15. Eric Dey, "Dimensions of Faculty Stress: A Recent Survey," *The Review of Higher Education* 17, no. 3 (1994): 305–22.

NOTES

16. Esther D. Rothblum, "Leaving the Ivory Tower: Factors Contributing to Women's Voluntary Resignation from Academia," *Frontiers* 10, no. 2 (1988): 14–17.

17. Etzkowitz et al., "Paradox of 'Critical Mass,'" 17.

18. Prieto-Dayard et al., 42. This sample was not broken down by discipline.

19. Dey.

20. Kim McDonald, "Many Female Astronomers Say They Face Sex Harassment and Bias," *Chronicle of Higher Education,* 13 February 1991, sec. A, p. 11.

21. Eric Dey, Linda Sax, and Jessica Korn, "Betrayed by the Academy: The Sexual Harassment of Women College Faculty" (paper presented at the Annual Meeting of the American Educational Research Association, New Orleans, La., April 1994): 1–20.

22. McDonald.

Explaining Women's Experiences in Academic Science

1. Albert Bandura, "Self-Efficacy: Towards a Unifying Theory of Behavioral Change," *Psychological Review* 84, no. 2 (1977): 191–215; Nancy E. Betz, "What Stops Women and Minorities from Choosing and Completing Majors in Science and Engineering?" (paper presented for the Science and Public Policy Seminar of the Federation of Behavioral, Psychological and Cognitive Sciences, 15 June 1990). Betz, among others, use Bandura's model.

2. Seymour and Hewitt, 392.

3. Another powerful explanatory model at the individual level is that of attribution. The most pertinent research tied to this is shows that women internalize failures (attributing it to their level of ability or effort) and externalize success (attributing it to the nature of the task or to luck). Most research reports that men internalize success and externalize failure. It has also been found that women who internalize success tend to attribute it to unstable causes (efforts) rather than stable ones (such as ability). For a review of this see Betz.

Making a Positive Difference for Women in Science

1. Roberta M. Hall and Bernice Reznick Sandler, *Women Winners* (Washington, D.C.: Association of American Colleges, 2nd ed., 1991), 2.

Institutional Response

1. Marsha L. Matyas and Shirley M. Malcolm, *Investing in Human Potential: Science and Engineering at the Crossroads* (Washington, D.C.: AAAS. Report, 1991), 9.

2. Sheila Tobias, "Gender Politics," *CSWP Gazette: Newsletter of the Committee on the Status of Women in Physics American Physical Society* 14, no. 1 (1994): 10–11.

3. David Targan, "Interim Report of the Brown University Sloan Program" (interim report to the Alfred P. Sloan Foundation, November 1994).

4. Sue V. Rosser and Cinda-Sue Davis "Programmatic and Curricular Interventions: What Do We Know?" (paper presented at the CURIES Conference on Women in Science, Mathematics and Engineering, May 1994); see also Brainard, *The Freshman Intervention Program*; Wiegand et al.

5. Matyas and Malcolm.

6. Paraphrase of Sheila E. Widnall, "AAAS Presidential Lecture: Voices from the Pipeline," *Science* 241 (1988): 1740–3.

Recommendations for Change

1. Seymour and Hewitt, 395.

2. Ibid., 393.

3. Ibid., 394.

4. Ibid., 398.

5. Uri Treisman, "Studying Students Studying Calculus: A Look at the Lives of Minority Mathematics Students in College,"*College Mathematics Journal* 23, no. 5 (1992): 362–72.

6. Maria A. Chacón et al., "Chicanos in California Postsecondary Education," *La Red/the Net* 65 (winter 1983): 3–23.

7. Seymour and Hewitt, 399–400.

8. Astin and Sax report that students achieve better grades in college if they work on campus.

9. Fay Ajzenberg-Selove, *A Matter of Choices: Memoirs of a Female Physicist* (New Brunswick, N.J.: Rutgers University Press, 1994), 22.

10. Etzkowitz et al., "Athena Unbound," 163–4.

11. Etzkowitz et al., "Athena Unbound," 173

12. Brainard, personal communication with author.

13. Widnall.

14. Etzkowitz et al., "Athena Unbound."

15. It is worth repeating: at present e-mail is not a totally private way of communication. Do not put anything in e-mail that you would not want to see in writing or have forwarded to the whole world.

16. Debra L. Nelson, James Campbell Quick, and Janice R. Joplin, "Psychological Contracting and Newcomer Socialization: An Attachment Theory Foundation," *Journal of Social Behavior and Personality: Special Issue on Handbook on Job Stress* 6, no. 7 (1991): 55–72.

17. Carol Eastman, presentation at the "Transitions for Women in Academia" program at the University of Washington, 3 May 1994. Eastman was then dean of the graduate school at the University of Washington.

18. Tobias.

19. Seymour and Hewitt, 399.

20. For some references on group learning see Bailey in AAUW, 72–73.

21. Michael G. Barbour, Jack H. Burk, and Wanna D. Pitts, *Terrestrial Plant Ecology,* 2nd ed. (Menlo Park, Cal., Benjamin/Cummings Pub. Co., 1987).

22. Hall and Sandler, 16.

23. Hollenshead et al., 17.

24. Tobias.

25. Tobias; Dresselhaus.

26. Hollenshead et al.

27. Bozeman, 20. While Patterson was referring to ethnic minority students, this advice is good for any department attempting to bring in previously underrepresented groups.

28. Fox.

29. Seymour and Hewitt, 402.

30. Merle Waxman, "Mentoring, Role Modelling, and the Career Development of Junior Science Faculty," *Journal of College Science Teaching* 22, no. 2 (1992): 124–27.

31. Nelson et al. The University of Washington has instituted this system campus-wide. Waxman (1992) recommends a "faculty advisor on professional growth and the promotion process" (126).

32. Targan, 1994.

33. Linda S. Wilson, "The Scientific Community at Crossroads: Discovery in a Cultural and Political Context" (paper presented at the Annual Meeting of the American Association for the Advancement of Science, February 1993), 12.

34. Seymour and Hewitt, 408.

35. Ibid., 409.

36. J. Butler, A. B. Ginorio, and B. Schmitz, roundtable discussion of course changes resulting from participation in curriculum integration project, "Different Voices," at the annual conference fo the National Association for Ethnic Studies, Seattle, Wash. (March 1989).

37. Dey, 320.

38. Strategy proposed by Garrison Sposito, as reported by Marsha L. Matyas and Linda S. Dix, eds., *Science and Engineering Programs: On Target for Women?* (Washington, D.C.: National Academy of Sciences, 1992).

39. Ibid.

40. Fox reports that women's participation in professional conferences' invited programs is lower than women's participation in the open programs, and that invited programs which included a woman among the organizers had a higher level of women's participation.

41. The National Council for Research on Women has a list of all women's caucuses in various professional organizations.

SELECTED BIBLIOGRAPHY

In addition to the rich bibliography on women and science represented by the endnotes for *Warming the Climate for Women in Academic Science,* the annotated bibliography below is offered to suggest the range of compelling new scholarship on women and science that has emerged, particularly in the last decade. The titles only hint at the developing sophistication, depth, and scope of new questions raised about gender, math, and science.

Bell-Scott, Patricia, ed. *Sage* 6, no. 2 (1989). Special issue: science and technology.
    This issue focuses on black women in science and technology. Sylvia T. Bozeman's article, "Black Women Mathematicians: In Short Supply," cited in Ginorio's text appears in this issue. There are also articles by Shirley Malcolm, Rosalyn Patterson, Evelyn Boyd Granville, and others.
Bleier, Ruth. *Science and Gender: A Critique of Biology and Its Theories on Women.* Elmsford, N.Y.: Pergamon, 1984.
    Bleier focuses on the role of scientific theory in defending the social status quo, especially with regard to biological theories used to support cultural beliefs that women are inferior and therefore meant to be subordinate.
———, ed. *Feminist Approaches to Science.* Elmsford, N.Y.: Pergamon, 1986.
    This collection addresses feminist methodology, feminist pedagogy, and the feminist critique of the natural sciences.
Farrant, Patricia, and Alice Miller, eds. *Initiatives: Journal of the National Association for Women in Education* 55, no. 2 (1993); no. 3 (1993). Special issue: gender equity in math and science, parts one and two.
    In a comprehensive collection of essays on women in math, science, and technology, this two-part series argues that retention, rather than recruitment, is the key to redressing the underrepresentation of women in math, science, and science-related fields. Many articles focus on diverse intervention programs that have been implemented and evaluated from K–12 to higher education.
Fausto-Sterling, Anne. *Myths of Gender: Biological Theories About Women and Men.* 2nd ed. New York: Basic Books, 1992.
    This book explores the role of cultural beliefs in creating and interpreting hypotheses about the biological basis of gender and behavior.
Haraway, Donna. *Primate Visions: Gender, Race and Nature in the World of Modern Science.* New York: Routledge, 1989.
    This volume describes the history of research on primates, its relation to theories about women, and how these theories were affected by cultural assumptions, the sex of the researchers, and the feminist critique of science.
Harding, Sandra G. *Whose Science? Whose Knowledge?: Thinking From Women's Lives.* Ithaca, N.Y.: Cornell University Press, 1991.
    This volume includes essays on feminist methodology and how we know what we know, including the social basis of scientific knowledge, and the role of individual perspective (feminist, person of color, lesbian, and others) in the creation of knowledge.
———, ed. *The "Racial" Economy of Science: Toward a Democratic Future.* Bloomington, Ind.: Indiana University Press, 1993.
    This collection of essays about science as cultural phenomenon discusses how science reinforces cultural beliefs about racial differences, how science in the Third World depends on the First World's political agenda, and applications of science, including reproductive technology, developmental agriculture, and environmentalism. This volume also explores how science might change to serve a democratic world community.
———, ed. *The Science Question in Feminism.* Ithaca, N.Y.: Cornell University Press, 1986.
    This edited volume contains essays on the philosophy of science. It focuses on what is distinctive about feminist research and the relationship between scientific inquiry and feminist inquiry.
Journal of Women and Minorities in Science and Engineering. New York: Begall House, Inc.
    This is a new journal edited by Carol J. Burger of the Women's Research Institute, Virginia Polytechnic Institute and State University, 10 Sandy Hall, Blacksburg, VA 24061–0038. Phone: 703/231–6296.
Keller, Evelyn Fox. *Reflections on Science and Gender.* New Haven, Conn.: Yale University Press, 1985.
    Fox Keller offers discourses on the role of gender for both the scientist and the subject of study, and the historical, psychological, and philosophical role of gender in science.
Kahle, Jane Butler, ed. *Women in Science.* Philadelphia: Falmer Press, 1985.
    This edited volume addresses the history of women in science, the current role of women in science, and obstacles women of all races face in their respective scientific fields.
Rosser, Sue Vilhauer. *Female-Friendly Science: Applying Women's Studies Methods and Theories to Attract Students.* 1st ed. Elmsford, N.Y.: Pergamon, 1990.
    These essays focus on feminist method and its role in pedagogy, especially with regard to increasing the numbers of women in science.

Schiebinger, Londa. *The Mind Has No Sex?* Cambridge, Mass.: Harvard University Press, 1991.

Schiebinger discusses the history of women's contributions to science and the historical and cultural influences that mold the course of scientific scholarship and knowledge.

Science 255, 13 March 1992: *Women in Science—Pieces of a Puzzle. Science* 260, 16 April 1993: *Gender and the Culture of Science. Science* 263, 11 March 1994: *Comparisons Across Cultures.*

These three special issues of the journal *Science* focus on women in science.

Traweek, Sharon. *Beamtimes and Lifetimes.* Cambridge, Mass.: Harvard University Press, 1988.

An anthropological study of high-energy physicists, this work exposes the role of science in shaping scientists' social culture and social culture's role in shaping science.

Tuana, Nancy. *The Less Noble Sex: Scientific, Religious, and Philosophical Conceptions of Woman's Nature.* Bloomington, Ind.: Indiana University Press, 1993.

Tuana explores the impact of metaphysical conceptions of the nature of women on science and how those values constrain the development of scientific theories. The book also posits what a science organized on more gender-equal values might look like.

———, ed. *Feminism and Science.* Bloomington, Ind.: University of Indiana Press, 1989.

This edited volume contains essays about how science is affected by and reinforces sex biases and the political, social and economic values of science as a social and cultural institution.

University of Wisconsin Women's Studies Librarian's Office. *History of Women and Science, Health and Technology: A Bibliographic Guide to the Professions and the Disciplines.* Madison, Wis.: self-published, 1994.

This guide contains chapters on the history of women and science, feminist perspectives on the ethics of care, and more. To obtain this guide write to: Wisconsin System Women's Studies Librarian's Office, 430 Memorial Library, 728 State Street, Madison, WI 53706. Although published in book form this guide is also available electronically through WISCINFO.WISC.EDU, the University of Wisconsin–Madison Gopher Server, and can be searched and downloaded by chapter. Alternatively, send e-mail to the women's studies librarian's office: WISWSL@MACC.WISC.EDU (Internet).

Zuckerman, Harriet, Jonathan R. Cole, and J. T. Bruer, eds. *The Outer Circle: Women in the Scientific Community.* New York: W. W. Norton and Co., 1991.

This collection includes theory, analysis, data, and interviews with successful women scientists, all addressing the experience of women in science. This volume examines why women scientists tend to publish less, receive fewer promotions, and earn less than their male counterparts, and identifies the barriers facing women who enter science.

Forthcoming

Arnold, Karen D. *Promises to Keep: Valedictorians Over Time.* San Francisco: Jossey-Bass, forthcoming.

Arnold discusses the Illinois Valedictorian Project cited in the text; the title is a working title and may change.

Davis, C. S., A. B. Ginorio, C. Hollenshead, B. Lazarus, and P. Rayman, eds. *The Equity Equation.* Forthcoming.

This collection includes presentations prepared for the CURIES/Sloan Foundation conference on women in science, mathematics, and engineering. All reports noted in the endnotes as coming from this conference will be included.

Seymour, Elaine, and Nancy Hewitt. *Talking About Leaving.* Boulder, Colo.: Greenhaven Press, forthcoming.

This volume studies students' reasons for staying in or leaving the sciences (cited in the text).

Spanier, Bonnie. *Im/partial Visions of Life: Gender and Ideology in Molecular Biology.* Bloomington, Ind.: Indiana University Press, forthcoming.

This forthcoming book is a feminist critique of the content of molecular biology. The title is a working title and may change.

RESOURCES

Organizations

American Association for the Advancement of Science (AAAS) Office of Opportunities in Science

1333 H Street, NW

Washington, DC 20005

Phone: 202/326–6680

Director: Shirley M. Malcolm, Head, Office of Opportunities in Science.

A national organization, AAAS covers many disciplines and publishes the journal *Science,* which occasionally devotes special issues to the topics of women in science and minorities in science.

American Association of University Women (AAUW) Education Foundation

111 Sixteenth Street, NW

Washington, DC 20036–4873

Phone: 202/728–7602

Fax: 202/872–1425

General Information/HELPLINE: 800/821–4364, ext. 67

Director: Tanya Hilton

This foundation is one arm of AAUW. They also have various fellowships and grants to support science education. AAUW local chapters throughout the U.S. run a program for girls called "Expanding Your Horizons," aimed at increasing girls' participation in science.

Association of Women in Science (AWIS)

1522 K Street, NW

Suite 820

Washington, DC 20005

Phone: 202/408–0742

Fax: 202/408–8321

Director: Catherine Jay Didion

A professional organization, AWIS promotes the participation of women in science; open to all. Local chapters exist throughout the United States with an active mentoring program.

Commission on Professionals in Science and Technology

1500 Massachusetts Avenue, NW

Suite 831

Washington, DC 20005

Phone: 202/223–6996

Fax: 202/223–6444

Director: Eleanor Babco, Acting Director

This group produces up-to-date and complete documentation on the participation and status of women and minorities in science, mathematics, and engineering.

National Council for Research on Women

530 Broadway at Spring Street, Tenth Floor

New York, NY 10012–3920

Phone: 212/274–0730

Fax: 212/274–0821

Director: Mary Ellen S. Capek, Executive Director

This organization maintains a list of all women's caucuses in various professional organizations, as mentioned in the endnotes. It is a national organization with Centers for Research on Women on campuses throughout the country.

National Network of Minority Women in Science
1333 H Street, NW
Washington, DC 20005
Phone: 202/326–6670
Fax: 202/371–9849
Director: Gloria Gilbert, National MWIS Coordinator
This national organization provides access to career information and educational opportunities for minority female students and promotes the professional advancement of minority women scientists and engineers. Fellowship programs both for education and professional growth are available.

Society of Women Engineers (SWE)
120 Wall Street
New York, NY 10005
Phone 212/509–9577; 800/666–1SWE (1793)
Director: Elaine P. Osterman, Executive Director
A national organization with local and student chapters, SWE provides outreach to support and increase the number of women engineers at the undergraduate, graduate and professional levels.

Women in Engineering Program Advocates Network (WEPAN)
1500 Massachusetts Avenue, NW
Suite 831
Washington, DC 20005
Phone: 317/494–5387
Fax: 317/496–1349
Internet: wiep@ecn.purdue.edu
Director: Suzanne Brainard, President
Founded in 1990 to increase the number of women who pursue careers in engineering by encouraging colleges and universities to initiate or expand women in engineering programs at the pre-college, undergraduate, and graduate levels, WEPAN is a national organization with regional centers

Electronic Resources

There are numerous electronic mail lists and bulletin boards relating to issues of women in science and technology as well as discipline specific lists (e.g. SYSTERS, a list for women in computer science). There are also numerous gopher sites and World Wide Web pages relating to women's issues.

Lists with LISTSERV, LIST PROC or COMSERV addresses are managed with automated software. To subscribe, send the following message to the address given: SUB <listname><Your name>, e.g. SUB FIST Nanette E. Jones. Send a similar message to lists with MAJORDOMO addresses, but omit your name unless otherwise instructed. For lists that do not have one of these types of addresses, be sure to include your name and e-mail address at the end of your message asking to subscribe, unless otherwise instructed. Another source for electronic forums are Usenet/VNEWS newsgroups. Access to Usenet varies slightly by university—ask the people at your institution for instructions.

If you need to contact the listowner of a list which is administered with LISTSERV, you only need to send a message: <list name>-<request>@<node>. See FIST below for an example.

Portions of the list below were taken from a document, "Gender-Related Electronic Forums," available through the WMST-L files, compiled by Joan Korenman, listowner of the women's studies list (WMST-L@umdd.umd.edu).

EDUCOM-W
LISTSERV@BITNIC (Bitnet) or LISTSERV@BITNIC.EDUCOM.EDU (Internet)
This list focuses on issues in technology and education that are of interest to women.

Feminists in Science and Technology (FIST)
FIST-REQUEST@FAMILY.HAMPSHIRE.EDU
FIST is an unmoderated list for discussion of feminism in science and technology. Send a message with "subscribe" in the first line.

RESOURCES

Gender, Science, Engineering, and Technology (gender-set)

mailbase@mailbase.ac.uk

Send the message: join gender-set <first name><last name>

This list for discusses research on gender differences in SET (science, engineering and technology) occupations and education, feminist science studies and philosophical critiques of SET.

Lesbians in Science (LIS)

LIS-REQUEST@KENYON.EDU

LIS is self-defined as an "international organization of dykes, practicing or interested in diverse sciences," as well as an e-mail list for discussions, resource and information sharing, and support. Women only.

National Organization for Gay and Lesbian Scientists and Technical Professionals (NOGLSTP)

NOGSLTP-REQUEST@ELROY.FPL.NASA.GOV

This is a discussion list for gay and lesbian scientists and professionals.

Young Scientists Network (YSN)

ysn-request@ren.salk.edu

YSN is a news digest for discussion of issues involving the employment of scientists, especially those just beginning their careers.

Women in Science and Engineering Network (WISENET)

LISTSERV@UICVM (Bitnet) or LISTSERV@UICVM.UIC.EDU (Internet)

This is a list for women in science, mathematics, and engineering.

Women Undergraduates in Science (WOMUNSCI)

Majordomo@freya.sc.umass.edu

WOMUNSCI is a moderated list for discussing the topic of increasing participation of undergraduate women in science. Membership is open to women undergraduates interested in science, college science educators, and administrators.

Other Resources

On most campuses there are committees, task forces, or commissions on women or gender which report to either the provost or faculty senate. If you are a faculty member, you may wish to serve on one of these. Most professional societies have a women's caucus. If you are a graduate student or faculty member, you may wish to investigate the women's caucus for the organization(s) you belong to. These committees and caucuses monitor the status of women in their institutions and organizations and often help set policy.

AA&U

Association of American Colleges and Universities
Program on the Status and Education of Women
1818 R Street, NW, Washington, DC 20009
202/387–3760